The Discursive Power of Memes in Digital Culture

Shared, posted, tweeted, commented upon, and discussed online as well as offline, internet memes represent a new genre of online communication, and an understanding of their production, dissemination, and implications in the real world enables an improved ability to navigate digital culture. This book explores cases of cultural, economic, and political critique levied by the purposeful production and consumption of internet memes. Often images, animated GIFs, or videos are remixed in such a way to incorporate intertextual references, quite frequently to popular culture, alongside a joke or critique of some aspect of the human experience. Ideology, semiotics, and intertextuality coalesce in the book's argument that internet memes represent a new form of meaning-making, and the rapidity by which they are produced and spread underscores their importance.

Bradley E. Wiggins is an Associate Professor and head of the media communications department at Webster Vienna Private University. His investigations of digital culture and discourse involve research on internet memes, social media, and fake news. Additional research includes game and simulation-based learning, intercultural and strategic communication.

Routledge Studies in New Media and Cyberculture

For more information about this series, please visit: https://www.routledge.com

The Discursive Power of Memes in Digital Culture

Ideology, Semiotics, and Intertextuality

Bradley E. Wiggins

Routledge
Taylor & Francis Group

LONDON AND NEW YORK

First published 2019
by Routledge

2 Park Square, Milton Park, Abingdon, Oxfordshire OX14 4RN
52 Vanderbilt Avenue, New York, NY 10017

Routledge is an imprint of the Taylor & Francis Group, an informa business

First issued in paperback 2020

Library of Congress Cataloging-in-Publication Data
Names: Wiggins, Bradley E., 1977– author.
Title: The discursive power of memes in digital culture: ideology, semiotics, and intertextuality / Bradley E. Wiggins.
Description: 1 Edition. | New York: Routledge, 2018. |
Series: Routledge studies in new media and cyberculture; 45
Identifiers: LCCN 2018056355 (print) |
LCCN 2018060207 (ebook)
Subjects: LCSH: Memes. | Digital communications. | Social media—Social aspects. | Intercultural communication.
Classification: LCC HM626 (ebook) | LCC HM626 .W564 2018 (print) | DDC 302.23/1—dc23
LC record available at https://lccn.loc.gov/2018056355

ISBN: 978-1-138-58840-0 (hbk)
ISBN: 978-0-367-66133-5 (pbk)

Typeset in Sabon
by codeMantra

For Harambe

Contents

x   *Contents*

List of Figures

List of Tables

Preface/Foreword

Spoiler alert: this isn't really a book about memes.

Well, it is. But, it also isn't.

It's a book about ideology, or more precisely, about what I'm calling *ideological practice*.

The central argument is that internet memes are discursive units of digital culture and that these units of discourse indicate an *ideological practice*. To be specific, I primarily refer to those internet memes which inhere some form or degree of critique, be it a critique of a politician, celebrity, social, cultural, or economic issue, etc. The *practice* of ideology occurs in the construction, comprehension, and furtherance of internet memes as units of discourse. Within construction, a difference exists between video and non-video internet memes. I place most analytical emphasis on the image-based internet memes as these are, arguably, the most pervasive and perhaps also the most malleable of all sub-genres of internet memes. Video memes (as well as animated forms such as GIFs) naturally also contain aspects of an *ideological practice*, but the role and degree of semiotics and intertextuality is limited proportionate to the presence of human speech. With human speech, analysis of such memes is best undertaken by following Shifman's (2013) memetic typology of content, form, and stance, whereby *stance* is primarily concerned with the tone and style of the communication as well as the *communicative function* following Jakobson's (1960) six functions of human speech communication. With regard to image-based memes, the absence of speech means the magnification of the visual-verbal mode of making meaning. Within image-based memes, the role of semiotics and intertextuality is elevated in the construction of meaning. For such memes, I have adjusted Shifman's typology and recast it as an *elaboration of the model* for the analysis of image-based memes. Yet to posit that meaning is constructed assumes an audience comprised of individuals capable to understand the message. I dedicate an entire chapter to the deliberation of *audience* with respect to memes, but for the purpose of this introduction while certain memes do in fact have an *audience* (be it *real* or *imagined*), the vast majority of critical memes inhere a directionality which addresses at least two groups, one which is positioned to '*get the joke*' and one which may be the target of the joke. In internet memes, semiotics, or more generally the study of meaning making (or how processes such as allegory, analogy, catachresis, juxtaposition, metaphor, metonymy, parody, pastiche, signification, simulation, symbolism, synecdoche, etc. are used to make meaning of reality), is an important facet to understand, especially given the proclivities of digital culture for rapidly consuming and sharing truncated forms of expression. Its relationship to intertextuality, or the bridging of one text with another text through citation, parody, reference, remix, etc., often overlaps especially with regard to understanding how meaning is constructed and for what purpose. Finally, the place of *ideological practice* coalesces as a meeting point for the semiotic and intertextual choices made in the construction and further spread of given internet memes. This is not to suggest that we need to concern ourselves with the *author* of a given meme and ascertain their identity in order to assign ideological meaning; rather, it is in the sharing, curation, and remixing, etc. of internet memes where ideological *practice* takes place. In digital culture, internet memes exist as a genre of online communication. Further, memes are also simultaneously artifacts emblematic of digital culture. Their production, consumption, and spread, address an agency within a social system and these are further enabled by memory traces in the tradition of Giddens' concept of *structuration*. Internet memes which address a real-world event or issue also imply a *media narrative*, which I clarify in greater detail in the chapter on Audience. In the last chapter, I posit that internet memes – again, especially those which incorporate a critical message (even though this normally always is accomplished also through the use of humor) – are a new form of artistic expression. Internet memes are a new form of art, and one that conceptually traces back to Dadaism, Surrealism, and related forms of art.

1 Dawkins Revisited

A Brief History of the Term Meme and Its Function

A socio-historical account of the term "meme" reveals a concept that has mutated since its introduction. By "mutated," I mean to emphasize the ways in which *meme-as-a-concept* has itself changed because of human interaction with the internet. Prior to exploring the similarities and important differences between Richard Dawkins' *meme* and its digital counterpart, the *internet meme*, it is best to review the term *meme* in general and chart its development since its inception.

Evolutionary biologist Richard Dawkins introduced the meme in his book *The Selfish Gene* and intended the meme to be a response to the gene-centric focus of evolution. Dawkins' motivation for the neologism was rooted in the sense that "[w]e need a name for the new replicator, a noun that conveys the idea of cultural transmission, or a unit of *imitation*" (1989, p. 182, italics in original text). This was ostensibly due to the need to conceptualize and verbalize the posited relationship between cultural and genetic transmission in society. Curiously, Dawkins cites the Greek word *mimeme* in his effort to create a new word. It is perhaps worth noting that *mimeme*, or μίμημα ("mīmēma") translates from Ancient Greek to mean "imitated thing". Dawkins suggests that a shorter, monosyllabic word such as '*meme*' better captures the linkage between culture and memory. In unambiguous terms, Dawkins (1989) writes that

> [j]ust as genes propagate themselves in the gene pool by leaping from body to body via sperms or eggs, so memes propagate themselves in the meme pool by leaping from brain to brain via a process which, in the broad sense, can be called imitation.
>
> (p. 192)

However, it is this conceptual standpoint of *imitation* which is critical in understanding the difference between the Dawkinsian meme and the internet meme. Not *mimeme* but rather *enthymeme* better captures the essence of internet memes as a digital phenomenon marked not by imitation but by the capacity to propose or counter a discursive argument through visual and often also verbal interplay; the emphasis here is on those internet memes which inhere a critical component of society, politics, etc. *Enthymeme* conceptually designates the fundamental differences between *meme* and *internet meme* from an orthographic as well as an etymological standpoint. Huntington (2017, p. 80) suggests that the "enthymeme lays out key points of an argument while leaving the conclusion of the argument unstated". Finnegan (2001, p. 143) argued that the *enthymeme* is

> an argument that is drawn from premises that do not need to be stated, 'since the hearer supplies it'...the enthymeme leaves space for the audience to insert its own knowledge and experience; it assumes an audience of judges capable of 'filling in the blanks' of an argument.

Similarly, Smith (2007, p. 122) concludes that enthymemes function in contemporary society not as the Aristotelian syllogism but rather as visual arguments that

> contain premises and conclusions that are merely probable, thus recognizing the differences that are common in human interactions. They call for judgment, and thus appeal emotionally and ethically as well as logically. Finally, their effectiveness depends on agreement between messenger and audience, discovered in the common opinions shaped by the contexts and culture of the people addressed.

A later section expounds on the differences between the Dawkinsian meme and the internet meme, but it is more conceptually clear to view the etymological inception of *meme*, with reference to its digital counterpart, as emanating from *enthymeme* and not simply an imitation of something as with *mimeme*.

To return to the meme, as described by Dawkins, and its internet counterpart, he envisioned the meme as a cultural unit (or idea) that sought replication for the purpose of its own survival. Ideas (or memes per Dawkins) are inherently selfish and virulent, competing to infect individual minds to use them as vehicles for replication. Dawkins' meme was generally conceived, including such examples as slogans, catch phrases, fashion, learned skills, and so on. The emphasis in all these examples of the Dawkinsian meme is clearly imitation, or an imitative force. According to Dawkins, catch phrases, popular songs, and fashion all persist through agential imitation and replication. Like genes, which are ubiquitous and essential to evolution, Dawkins saw the gene as a metaphor for the meme. By describing evolution as a cultural phenomenon – not a biological phenomenon – Burman (2012) suggests Dawkins' purpose was to "[redefine] the fundamental unit of selection in evolutionary biology" (p. 77). For Dawkins, the meme served as a catalyst for cultural jumps in human evolution, much like a gene served to further biological evolution. Memes are the mediators of cultural evolution. Within the decade following Dawkins' work in the 1970s, the gene ceased being simply a metaphor for meme. Gene and meme became synonymous. Hofstadter (1983, p. 18) took Dawkins' metaphor and imagined it more literally:

> Memes, like genes, are susceptible to variation or distortion – the analogue of mutation. Various mutations of a meme will have to compete with one another, as well as with other memes, for attention, that is, for brain resources in terms of both space and time devoted to that meme.

Moreover, Hofstadter notes further competition among memes because of aural and visual transmission, suggesting that memes unlike genes will compete "for radio and television time, billboard space, newspaper and magazine column-inches and library shelf-space". It is worth noting here the close parallel to the infrastructure of the internet and human interaction. The draw on attention ("brain resources in terms of both space and time") is relevant to our contemporary reliance on digital and online forms of communication regardless of internet memes per se.

By 1995, Burman (2012) writes, "the meme had become active and non-metaphorical" (p. 89). The understanding of *meme* was a given obvious item of knowledge thus shaping our assumptions of it and how it is to be understood at a time when the current *internet meme* was years away. In a sense, the Dawkinsian *meme* – the concept itself as a spreadable idea – became a prime example of its explicitly articulated definition, in the tradition of Dawkins, which is to *infect* language and thought, replicating itself within the minds and languages of individuals for the sole purpose of replication. Although the meme has a long history of usage tied to linguistics, psychology, and philosophy, the contemporary meaning of meme is much different. Its current meaning describes a *genre of communication*, not a unit of cultural transmission. Interestingly, scholarship on memes has historically relied on an "epidemiological model" (Weng, Flammini, Vespignani, & Menczer, 2012, p. 6). As such it is a metaphorical model that confines the meme conceptually within biology and evolution. Specifically, from an epidemiological stance, the meme spreads much like a disease. This, of course, echoes Dawkins' own initial treatment of meme as well as the way in which the field of memetics responded to Dawkins' neologism. For example, Blackmore's (2000) book *The Meme Machine* argued for an actual science of memetics, all in response to Dawkins' simple but necessary decision to offer a cultural corollary to the biological gene. Similarly, and following Dawkins, Aunger (2002, p. 2) extends the Dawkinsian perspective of the biological connection by stating that memes represent "an idea that becomes commonly shared through social transmission". Kien (2013, p. 554) refers to Aunger (2002) in his excoriation of media researchers who, in his view, have "abused [the] term in its reduction by media studies to mere internet phenomena". While Aunger deliberately emphasized the biological in his work, researchers such as Kien (2013) and Milner (2012) needlessly extend the reliance on Dawkins and the biological metaphor, a process which fails to grasp the ideational argumentation afforded by internet memes. The epidemiological approach serves as a false analogy for the digital understanding and usage of memes by placing the power of their spread in the memes and ignoring agency.

Similarly, Jenkins (2009, para. 18) states that "the idea of the meme and the media virus, of self-replicating ideas hidden in attractive, catchy content we are helpless to resist – is a problematic way to understand cultural practices". Jenkins proceeds with an explanation of the role of agency as critical to understanding cultural change, but the argument suffers from an implicit presumption that *meme* necessarily means what Dawkins originally suggested. While Jenkins is correct to assert that memes do not replicate themselves, the argument suffers in stating that individuals are not susceptible to *viral* media, memes, or otherwise. This view emerges from an epidemiological assumption that memes, like a media virus, infect people, making them susceptible to influence. This perhaps accidental reliance on Dawkins' biological metaphor prevents the opportunity to reveal that the Dawkinsian definition does not apply to internet memes given their capacity to function as visual arguments and not simply "attractive, catchy content". It is important to explore the distinction between *viral media* and *internet memes* in greater detail if only to provide clarity to my insistence on viewing memes as visual arguments.

Memes and Viral Media

When comparing internet memes to viral media (or the capacity for media content, such as texts, images, hashtags, etc. to spread massively in online spaces often for relatively short periods of time), the tendency is to posit that due to the agency involved in the production and dissemination of internet memes, they are viewed as qualitatively different from viral media.

Typically, the distinction is explained with an emphasis on the manner by which change, imitation, remix, modification, etc. is perceived, and this is articulated as the origin of the distinction. For example, many researchers on this topic might cite *Gangnam Style*, a music video featuring South Korean musician Psy. The video has been viewed over 3 billion times since it was uploaded to YouTube on July 12, 2012. In this example, the argument goes that the *views* of a video do not count as a modification or remix but rather indicates *virality*.

Indeed, Shifman (2011) lightly distinguishes between *viral* and what she terms *memetic* videos in her analysis of a series of YouTube videos. She demarcates *viral* as "a clip that spreads to the masses via digital word-of-mouth mechanisms *without significant change* [italics in original]" (2011, p. 190). With *memetic* video, Shifman asserts that "a different structure of participation" incorporates "two main mechanisms in relating to the 'original' memetic video", namely imitation and remix (2011, p. 190). Shifman takes *viral* and *memetic* and equates them with Jenkins' term *spreadable media* but acknowledges that the term still necessitates some clarity. However, subsuming *viral* and *memetic* under *spreadable media* suggests an effort to refine the specific toward the general. Equating *spreadable media* with a derivative is counterproductive, since doing so assumes a conceptual alignment.

Further, and to borrow an important perspective from the field of sociolinguistics and linguistic anthropology, Varis and Blommaert (2015, pp. 35–36) understand Shifman's (2011) argument as emphasizing "the absence of signification change to the sign itself to distinguish virality from 'memicity': memes, as opposed to viral signs, would involve changes to the sign itself". Here, Varis and Blommaert understand internet memes as *signs*, which in semiotics is the quality of a thing to communicate meaning. As noted in the second chapter and following the definition of semiotician Umberto Eco, the sign is "produced with *the intention of* communication, that is, in order to transmit one's representation or inner state to another being" (1984, p. 16). The core of Varis and Blommaert's argument is that when considering activities associated with social semiotics (processes of meaning making across groups in society), the distinction between *viral* and *memetic* is less tenable than Jenkins or Shifman has considered. Rather this sociolinguistic argument is that to share information on Facebook, for example, is a form of "re-entextualization", or "meaningful communicative operations that demand different levels of agency and creativity of the user" (2015, p. 41). Additionally, Varis and Blommaert (2015) assert that such an act involves "re-semiotization", which suggests that every repetitive expression of a sign invariably "involves an entirely new set of contextualization conditions and thus results in an entirely 'new' semiotic process, allowing new semiotic modes and resources to be involved in the repetition process" (p. 36). Further, they argue that a Facebook post that generates tens of thousands of reactions does not mean that each person who reacted actually read the post. Similarly, a study conducted on Twitter revealed that approximately 59% of URLs shared were not actually clicked on at all (Gabielkov, Ramachandran, Chaintreau, & Legout, 2016, p. 8, in Wiggins, 2017). Thus, the main counterargument offered by Varis and Blommaert resides in the perspective that a piece of media content, such as a selfie, a looped video, or an image-macro, does not need to be altered in the way commonly expressed by researchers on memes because of the process of re-entextualization.

Bridging the Viral Divide

In an effort to bridge both perspectives, suppose a given selfie is uploaded to Instagram and attains a massive level of reactions. In this case, the selfie has led to some degree of *virality*; however, it is not an internet meme in the sense that it offers some form of visual argument. It is, nevertheless, an iteration of the Dawkinsian variant as a selfie exists as an idea that is executable and imitable. Additionally, it is also a sign given its communicative function, and as such exists as another genre of communication. Thus, following Eco's (1984) definition of sign and Varis and Blommaert's (2015) suggestion that internet memes are semiotic signs, all forms of mediated content – whether they 'go *viral*' or not – that represent or transmit meaning, can also be viewed as semiotic signs. However, signs which inhere a visual argument achieved through an expression of ideological practice and constructed semiotically and often intertextually are the category of internet memes examined in this work. Whether an individual wishes to view all such content as memes or viral media, or semiotic signs, etc. is a personal choice. It is my contention that understanding the capacity for certain digital messages to argue a perspective visually constitutes an acknowledgement of the thing as an internet meme. The importance of such an action leads to opportunities to understand the ideology expressed, audience(s) addressed, identities constructed or negotiated, the degree to which media narratives are incorporated into the message, etc. In other words, their construction, curation, consumption, etc. are what should concern us, not questions of their epidemiological but rather their discursive power.

Scholarship on internet memes tends to address the inherent meaning within a meme or series of memes or may emanate from a specific event or be used as a discursive tool to express irony, for example. However, these attempts rarely, if ever, address the ideological interrelationship of semiotic and intertextual ramifications on meaning conveyed by the meme itself but also what its creation and curation say about the individuals, groups, etc. using them to engage in discursive practices. This book endeavors to introduce an understanding of internet memes through a conceptual prism of ideology, semiotics, and intertextuality

Memes as a Cultural Commodity

To be explicit, memes are no different than any other cultural commodity. The acquisition, display, desire for, and even knowledge of commodities communicates something about *us* in terms of our relationship to them and to each other. Communication is in essence inescapable. Further, individuals enact social relationships with and through memes because individuals are interpellated, or addressed, by the social system they inhabit (or with which they identify). Accordingly, individuals articulate their opinions, views, etc. of an issue in a specific way linked to a particular ideological practice. This is communicated through a deliberate semiotic construction of meaning that is mutually intelligible to one's perceived group to reify the social structure, itself recursively reconstituted through human–internet interaction. Accordingly, with *ideology,* I refer primarily to Althusser and Zizek; with *semiotics,* I am drawing on Eco, Hodge, and Barthes; and with *intertextuality,* I refer to the work of Kristeva, Barthes, as well as to related concepts. The subsequent chapter elucidates the conceptual core of the title of this work more extensively.

Memes and Culture

As noted, Richard Dawkins originally proposed the term as a cultural corollary to the gene. While the term is useful in understanding cultural transmission of practice, beliefs, customs, expressions, modes of behavior, nonverbal cues, etc., it is problematic when discussing the digital counterpart to Dawkins' cultural corollary. First, it is essential to investigate, at least on a preliminary level, what constitutes culture. Raymond Williams (1981) suggests that the word *culture* fundamentally refers to agriculture, the cultivation of crops to sustain human life. Indeed, to understand culture even from the most critical point of view requires the acknowledgement that the existential aspect of a species, such as humanity, necessitates a mode or method of sustaining itself and to do so reliably and systematically. Thus, when we speak of a culture, counterculture, pop culture, mass culture, hybrid culture, co-culture, sub-culture, etc., what is embedded within that concept is a shared understanding that all cultures are the result (that is in-progress and evolving systems of interacting, producing, co-creating meaning, etc.) of achieving a cultivated status making a person *cultivated* and *cultured.*

Further, from Williams' perspective on culture in general, it is imperative to emphasize that culture is lived; it is generated by individuals and groups who produce behaviors, texts, etc. as a consequence of living their lives. Dawkins is to be applauded for contributing a social concept, the *meme,* to suggest a way to communicate about how cultures retain knowledge of their practices. Linguistically, the term accomplishes a serious and challenging feat: the Dawkinsian meme enables the conceptualization of concrete (songs, fashions, architecture, etc.) as well as deeply abstract (god, freedom, supernatural, etc.) ideational characteristics of expressions of a given culture, in terms of what it produces in order to constitute itself, recursively. If culture is in fact generated and lived by individuals, the knowledge that enables that understanding harkens back to the initial implication of culture as the systemic affordance of enacting cultivation through *agriculture* (here I imply also Williams' understanding of the term, as discussed earlier). Thus, from Dawkins' point of view, the meme represents the success of cultural transmission and adoption. But what does this have to do with internet memes?

It Doesn't Meme What You Think

This is precisely the point where distinction between the Dawkinsian meme and the internet meme is so necessary. In academic as well as general discussions and writings, from mainstream news media to high-ranked peer-reviewed journals, understanding of the term meme seems haphazard at best. From this larger or broader usage of the term, *meme* refers generally to virtually all mediated content that spreads virally online. Appropriating Dawkins' term from this point of view, any image with text, for example, must or could be a meme. Furthermore, labelling digital mash-ups with the moniker *memes* ignores the opportunity to explore the diversity in expressions and meaning-making accomplished online.

Fundamentally, it is problematic to assume an analogous relationship between the Dawkinsian and the digital term because this ignores the discursive aspect of internet memes. Finally, what Dawkins describes with *meme* as the ideational movement of thoughts and concepts from brain to brain in the form of imitation fails to relate to the complex and multifaceted ways in which content is created, spread, etc. online.

Memes and Internet Memes

The association of Dawkins' term (meme) with its online counterpart is dubious given the degree to which internet memes differ in terms of their formation, spread, but most importantly due to the desperate need of human–computer interaction to further their development. In fact, Dawkins himself acknowledged that the internet meme is a "hijacking of the original term" he proposed in *The Selfish Gene*. Dawkins (2013, n.p.) claims that:

> [T]he very idea of the meme, has itself mutated and evolved in a new direction. An internet meme is a hijacking of the original idea. Instead of mutating by random chance, before spreading by a form of Darwinian selection, internet memes are altered deliberately by human creativity. In the hijacked version, mutations are designed – not random – with the full knowledge of the person doing the mutating.

Mutation and hijacking, central to Dawkins' claim, highlight the social and cultural elements necessary to my approach to defining, conceptualizing, and theorizing about what we come to view as internet memes. In what follows, I review several other perspectives on internet memes, draw differences between the Dawkinsian and the digital version, and then I introduce the definition of *internet meme* operationalized for the purpose of this work.

Often the meme as message is more a visual argument than simply a joke that is replicated. In only two ways do memes align conceptually and practically with internet memes, that is (1) in terms of the demand on human attention and that (2) individuals should be able to reproduce them without much difficulty. This distinction offers a clarity which is lacking in the academic discourse on internet memes as a definitive offspring from the work of Dawkins. However, Shifman (2013) notes rather astutely that as a concept, the *meme* in the tradition of Dawkins consistently received ire and criticism in academia but has "enthusiastically been picked up by Internet users" (p. 365). Shifman (2014) differentiates her conceptualization of *meme* as compared to Dawkins' view by writing that "instead of depicting the meme as a single cultural unit that has propagated well, I treat memes as groups of content units" (p. 343). With this she means that internet memes demonstrate subject-matter awareness but that this awareness can be articulated in an array of internet meme sub-genres. Furthermore, Shifman (2013) explores areas related to memes such as diffusion of innovation studies but notes that these often overlook "the complexity and richness that may be ascribed to the [meme] concept" (p. 367). Accordingly, she returns to Dawkins in her introduction of what she calls a typology of memetic dimensions. Shifman (2013) posits that internet memes are best viewed not as single ideas, thus deviating from a rigid interpretation of the Dawkinsian variant, but rather as "*groups* of content items that were created with awareness of each other and share common characteristics" (p. 367). Shifman's typology, to be discussed and extended in a later section, is comprised of three memetic dimensions, namely *content*, *form*, and *stance*. These dimensions are often used to analyze video memes, and it is in that practice when compared to other meme sub-genres that the third element of her typology *stance* necessitates adjustment especially with regard to image-based internet memes. I suggest further that internet memes are not merely *content items* and thus simply replicators of culture but are rather visual arguments, which are semiotically constructed with intertextual references to reflect an ideological practice.

The internet meme differs from/compares with the (cultural corollary) meme in the following ways. First, memes (as in Dawkins' original concept, extrapolated later by Susan Blackmore and others) are culturally based. As noted above all aspects of culture, everything that it enables and all that enables it with the exception of the biological (as this is then the realm of the gene), is a meme. For example, the ways in which the *kiss* is negotiated across cultures, enacted in certain situations, but avoided or greatly emphasized or sought after or altered in other situations is a meme in the strictest sense following Dawkins. A male person may be greeted with a *kiss* or two on the cheek(s) by another male in one culture but the very same action would or could be misconstrued and misinterpreted or possibly even marginalized and penalized in another culture. Yet, the *kiss* remains knowable, recognizable; it is a representation of a cultural practice connected to many different meanings but largely referring to a finite set of categories of enacting relations between people. This is the essence of Williams' sentiment that culture is generated by the individuals who live in it and are simultaneously engaged in co-creating shared forms of meaning. At this level, we can speak definitively of a meme as a cultural corollary of the gene. Dawkins essentially separates the human experience into two distinct but related modes: a biological gene that furthers, by replication, selection, or rejection, certain information that is passed on for the purpose of species survival or change. Similarly, the meme largely succeeds isomorphically in its imitative nature, its characteristic of being at once knowable and reproducible is essential to its existence and to our ability to speak about its function. From this standpoint, it is less helpful to continually rely on Dawkins' concept of the *meme* when discussing the latest use of (internet) memes to criticize a politician, parody an entertainer, or to express irony or sarcasm. References to Dawkins and his term *meme* should be contextualized in such a way that clearly shows that the digital counterpart is distinct. Dawkins implies this when he speaks of the internet meme as a *hijacking* of the original concept (see Chapter 3 for more details). His use of the term *hijacking* hints at agency and implies human–computer interaction for the purpose of communicating, not with the computer, but with other humans accordingly.

Further distinctions between meme and internet meme center on the argument that the former does not require electronic, digital, etc. or other mediated forms of communication, nor does a meme require mutual intelligibility of language. The former point is likely obvious but for the understanding of internet memes and their use in online spaces it is essential to examine the various communicative tools (media) necessary for their creation and dissemination. The latter point is perhaps less obvious or possibly a presumed mistake on my part. First, I do not suggest that we introduce a new term to replace *internet meme,* but I think it is quite important to know that if an online audience, whether real or imagined, is to understand a given internet meme mutual intelligibility of language is required. As in the example earlier of a *kiss* understood differently across cultures and genders, it is not important to know the specific changes or the reasons why differences are indeed perceived and knowable, but one still understands the *kiss* (as a Dawkinsian meme) regardless of whether one knows the particular cultural context. Thus, it is not essential for mutual intelligibility of a *kiss* as a form of nonverbal linguistic expression across cultures. However, with the example of an internet meme that compares someone to Voldemort, this requires and implies (at least at a basic level) that the individual compared to the Harry Potter villain is not portrayed in a positive light (not to mention the required knowledge of popular culture references).

More sophisticatedly, the implication is that a reference to a particular part of popular culture is made to suggest that the real-world referent (be it an actor, politician, or a random individual) is worthy of such criticism. To understand such a reference requires some other area of knowledge. Naturally, the use of popular culture referents assists in maximizing the reception of the meme's message – but this cannot be universally applied in the example of the *kiss*, as discussed earlier. An individual may recognize that they are presented with what is commonly understood as an *internet meme* and may *get the joke*, but popular culture references or even *intermemetic* references (memes that refer to other memes) may not be completely understood. Admittedly, this may not be essential for the consumption and transmission of the message. However, with regard to politically charged or socially polarizing issues, an individual requires understanding of the context of the referent in order for the internet meme to achieve salience. More specific examples are offered in subsequent chapters, although this chapter concludes with an internet meme that is politically nuanced and that discussion offers further depth to my reasoning expressed here.

The *internet meme is hereby defined* as a remixed, iterated message that can be rapidly diffused by members of participatory digital culture for the purpose of satire, parody, critique, or other discursive activity. An *internet meme* is a more specific term for the various iterations it represents, such as image macro memes, GIFs, hashtags, video memes, and more. Its function is to posit an argument, visually, in order to commence, extend, counter, or influence a discourse. Naturally this can occur within humorous contexts; however, humor is merely the surface-level entry point for social salience. Digging deeper, one can view the argument within the meme which is usually if not always representative of an ideological practice.

Memes and the Role of Remix

For memes in the tradition of Dawkins, their reproduction is not dependent upon remix, but does require mimicry, parody, or imitation. For a thing to be imitated, mimicked, or parodied, it is essential for a person to view and understand some form of activity and to understand how to reproduce that same behavior in a similar or slightly altered way for some effect. Remix, on the other hand, requires a similar process especially with regard to parody. Indeed, parody is a remixing of, for example, a real-world event staged in a way to induce laughter for a socio-culturally critical effect. For internet memes, however, remixing means something slightly different. Parody can still be involved in the remixing of a real-world referent and an intertextual reference to popular culture, for example, but it is not essential hence the need to acknowledge a distinction between remix and parody in internet memes. For internet memes, *remix* means that an idea about a particular person (Russian President Vladimir Putin or Patrick Stewart as Captain Picard from *Star Trek: The Next Generation*), event (the 2016 U.S. Presidential election or the fall of the Berlin Wall), movement (#lovewins or #metoo), place (Syria or a restaurant), etc. must be maintained through the various iterations of the meme while simultaneously accompanied by changed or modified portrayals of the same content.

Remix in internet memes is an indispensable component of their structure and their capacity for consumption and reproduction. Just for fun, here is an example from the popular television series *The Walking Dead*. The *Look at the Flowers* internet meme depicts the character Carol pointing a gun and looking emotionally affected by the anticipated outcome of her action, namely the shooting of a young girl. If this meme is deployed as a comment to a Facebook thread in which a person disagrees with the content posted, instead of articulating this disagreement or frustration in text-only (verbal language) expressions, the use of the meme as a form of visually remixed communication offers an interesting alternative to verbal language. The image of Carol pointing the gun can simply be inserted – with or without text – and the core meaning is sustained (provided the individuals share mutual intelligibility of the particular contextual item in question) but is at once remixed, meaning its deployment can be as a comment, as a part of another visual frame (perhaps positioned next to an image of a controversial political figure), or inserted within another intertextual frame (perhaps positioned next to an image of a character from a television series or film who may be widely seen as annoying, such as the character Barb from *Stranger Things* or Jar Jar Binks from the *Star Wars* prequels). Remixing occurs as a necessary step in the realization of an internet meme's process of generating and sustaining meaning which is co-constructed between the (unimportant or unknowable) author of a given internet meme and the audience consuming the message. As described, the process is more dynamic than simple imitation.

You Can't Touch My Meme

Another difference is that Dawkinsian memes may take different forms but are usually intangible. Dawkins (1989) cites "tunes, catch-phrases, fashions, ways of making pots or building arches" as examples of this point (p. 192). Thus, it is not the pot or arch itself that is the meme, it is the culturally shared knowledge that enables the creation of a pot or arch. In contrast, internet memes are digitally based but require human action/reaction and as such are a genre of communication in online social networks. As a genre of communication – to be discussed in greater detail in Chapter 3 – it is unsurprising that internet memes function also as artifacts of the system that created them, namely participatory digital culture. As noted, internet memes require remix but are also heavily dependent, one might even say obsessed with parody and intertextuality and even intermemetic-referentiality (memes that refer to other memes). The procedural difference between remix and parody again is that remix is more a necessary process for the internet meme to function as such, regardless of its communicative intent, whereas with any parody, while also implying some level of imitation and generally speaking, humor, or more precisely satire, an individual already more or less knows the structure without having to identify with or know the content in order for it to be perceived as a parody. For internet memes, remix is an overarching structural requirement absent of any real semiotic information beyond the basic understanding that a core idea or notion is maintained thematically but may not be maintained in similar visual ways. Also, internet memes are digital, and no known non-digital or non-online example exists – with the exception of internet memes that have become physically commodified in the form of wearable items, such as t-shirts which may feature a structural aspect of a popular meme (such as the *Doge* meme or the *Y U No Guy* meme, whose visages may be viewed more properly as "old memes"). One possible exception is when internet memes are deployed in spaces where they are not native inhabitants such as part of a marketing campaign or when used by a government to attack its political opponents (Pearce & Hajizada, 2014). Internet memes necessitate human agency whose identity is unimportant (Here I do not suggest that *identity* itself is unimportant, an entire chapter is dedicated to the issue of *identity* and internet memes. Rather, I simply mean that the first step is to acknowledge the role of human agency in the production and dissemination of memes, and that the individual identities of all those involved are less important than the function of agency in a social system, especially one that incorporates, perhaps even necessitates digital technologies for communication purposes). In only two ways do Dawkinsian memes and internet memes compare well: both require attention and must be reproducible.

Attention and Reproducibility

Dawkins used the term *replicator* when discussing the process of genetic reproduction and also in reference to memes as the cultural corollary to the gene in the sense that by replicating something that already exists it can also exist. Yet as Dawkins notes (1989), not all genes replicate successfully and that this is the same for memes (p. 194). Dawkins states that memes must fundamentally possess three characteristics analogous to his discussion of the capacity for genetic replication.

Longevity, fecundity, and fidelity are each prerequisites for memes, per Dawkins. Longevity suggests a temporal aspect, and Dawkins admits that this is not important in terms of a particular copy of a meme but that memes exist at a particular time and can go out of fashion quickly or gradually. It is this last point at which Dawkins' term *longevity* makes sense in the comparison between memes and internet memes. Internet memes are often created in direct response to an event as a discursive way to add commentary or to argue a position, but the topic itself may eventually fade, the *function* of the internet meme does not. The temporal aspect afforded by longevity suggests that for internet memes, a particular reference to a person – such as the *Salt Bae* internet meme – may achieve virality due to the *popularity* of the meme itself but the remixing of a meme to incorporate another figure (Xi Jinping, Donald Trump, Theresa May, Bernie Sanders, Viktor Orban, etc.) adds to the potential for a particular meme to experience longevity.

Fecundity, upon first glance, appears to have greater importance than longevity consistent with Dawkins in terms of a meme's capacity for being spread. Again, though, this comparison to Dawkins' biological-cultural dialectic is tiresome since a given internet meme, such as the Trump executive order animated GIFs or the *Salt Bae* meme, is not particularly fecund, in the biological sense of being bountiful, fertile, productive, prolific, etc. Viewing a particular meme or a sub-genre of memes as fecund adds little to the discussion. Rather, it is important to delve deeper into the constitutive elements toward an understanding of the social semiotics embedded within a meme that translate into mass appeal and virality.

Fidelity suggests that memes (the Dawkins variant) should have an accurate, conjugal faithfulness to its particular referent. Dawkins admits he is "on shaky ground" with that assertion given that when one idea passes to another person it probably changes a bit, is tweaked or modified to suit that person's needs or worldview (1989, p. 194). Fidelity also relates to internet memes in that should a meme be altered, such as when new text or images are inserted, its particular function is likely maintained. For example, if a real-world event prompts a person to share memes, certain textual and visual elements will be chosen to maintain the sentiment linked to the event. Visually, this can differ in terms of popular culture references, for example, but conceptually fidelity is maintained.

The main distinction between Dawkins' meme and its digital counterpart is in the nature of their relationship, namely that *meme* is the umbrella concept, under which *internet meme* is merely an example. The internet phenomenon known commonly as memes is a type of Dawkinsian meme. Just as a person would not say *a tool is a type of spoon*, we should avoid assuming parity between internet memes and Dawkins' term, as alluded to by Shifman (2013) but I feel that especially given the *discursive power* of memes in online spaces, it is imperative for academics to realize the limitations of relying on the Dawkinsian perspective.

An Elaboration of Shifman's Typology of Memetic Dimension

The choice to analyze internet memes signifies their importance – either real or imagined – in terms of discursive practice within digital culture. One typology was developed in response to one particular video meme. Specifically, Shifman (2013) developed a tripartite typology consisting of **content** (what a meme conveys in terms of ideas and ideologies), **form** (what she calls the "physical incarnation of the message", but what I will adjust to mean the *memetic category of utility*), and **stance** (which "depicts the ways in which addressers position themselves in relation to the text, the linguistic codes, the addressees, and other potential speakers") (p. 367). With respect to Shifman's original intention for the typology to be used in analyzing internet memes, the tendency has been to use it in examining video memes. However, it is its application to non-video memes where it appears necessary to elaborate on the typology.

To be clear, Shifman's (2013) typology is an excellent starting point, but the dimension *stance* reveals an opportunity for elaboration of the typology which I will henceforth refer to as a model for meme analysis. In Table 1.1 below, I offer Shifman's original definition of the model and its constitutive elements with my extensions of these in truncated form. Following the table, I expound on specific examples as to why and how the model is to be view differently with non-video memes. To be clear, my elaboration is not a detraction of Shifman's model; rather, it strengthens the analytical viability and utility of the model for the wide swath of meme sub-genres. Concordantly, the primary driving force of this work – ideology, semiotics, and intertextuality – emerge more obviously in my elaboration of the model.

With respect to form, not all categories are equal in terms of the interpretability using the model in its original articulation. With video memes, stance is usefully viewed as a conduit for analyzing speech acts; mnemonically, it is helpful to consider that when analyzing video memes, stance relies heavily on the presence of speech. With other non-video examples, stance is joined by content inexorably due to the relationship between the expression of ideology and the manner by which meaning-making is accomplished without speech acts, thus emphasizing (or elevating the importance of) the role of semiotics and intertextuality in non-video memes.

With image-macros or inserted image memes such as *Salt Bae, White Woman Calls Cops* (also known as the *BBQ Becky* meme), *Salman Trump Orb, Netanyahu Power Point Template, Twilight Zone Trump, Gay Clown Putin, Puigdemont Catalonia, Erdogan (I want this meme arrested)* etc., the merging of content and stance must be emphasized. Content and stance merge given that the conveyance of ideas and ideologies occurs within deliberate semiotic and intertextual construction, especially with the absence of human speech.

Table 1.1 Elaboration of Memetic Typology

	Content	Form	Stance
Shifman (2013)	*Ideas and ideologies conveyed in a specific text*	*Physical incarnation of the message, perceived through our senses*	*Ways in which addressers position themselves in relation to the text; users decide to imitate a certain position that they find appealing or may use an utterly different discursive orientation*
Elaboration of model	*Unavoidable, inevitable as an aspect of communication which is rarely if ever accidental;* **inheres nature of ideological practice,** *with memes absent of human speech merges with stance*	*Neutral;* **memetic category of utility:** *video, GIF, image-macro, image inserted in another image, verbal text, hashtag, etc.*	*Loaded with meaning, charged; with* **memes absent of human speech,** *role of* **semiotic and intertextual construction of meaning** *is heightened, merges with content*

It is especially with image-based memes that ideological practice sig-nifies the relationship between content and stance and that this merg-ing is recursively constituted through agential interaction and memetic production. Stance becomes the location of semiotic and intertextual meaning alongside a certain ideological practice. It may be tempting to conclude that content houses the intertextual reference, but this would ignore the discursive power of individuals using memes to advance a particular position or issue which is the essence of ideological practice constructed through semiotic and intertextual choices.

Shifman (2013) extends stance, referring to it as a "very broad category" and draws on "concepts from discourse and media studies" by introduc-ing three subordinately constitutive components, namely participation structures ("who is able to participate and how"), keying (or "the tone and style of communication as defined by Goffman (1974)"), and com-municative functions (which draws on the work of Jakobson (1960) who identified six functions of human communication) (p. 367). Each of these components are especially helpful when analyzing video memes but when examining image-based memes, the absence of human speech acts suggests an alternative emphasis. It is not my intention to devalue Shifman's original typology; however, when applied to a variety of meme sub-genres again with special emphasis on image-based memes, the role of stance requires elaboration. Indeed, the connection between content and stance is already present in video memes but is more pronounced – necessarily so – with memes that are devoid of human speech acts, especially when the meme is constructed as a critical response to real-world occurrence.

With image memes, semiotics and intertextuality require further consideration. First, semiotics within stance refers to the visual cues constructed to convey a specific meaning; this is distinct from Shifman's (2013) original articulation of content which is concerned with the ideas and ideologies conveyed due to the poverty of the image to express itself in human speech. Rather, a semiotic elaboration within stance means that the role of metaphor, metonymy, juxtaposition, bricolage, pastiche, synecdoche, etc. is asserted due to the lack of human speech. Second, intertextuality seems an obvious choice for content; however, I posit that it must be situated in stance due to the "ways in which addressers position themselves in relation to the message" (Shifman, 2013, p. 367). Thus, different users will deploy different references to different (imagined) audiences. Intertextuality resides in stance due to the discursive function inherent in the remixing of image and referents for meaning-making. With the result of its function leading to meaning, the connection to semiotics should be clear. The bridge between stance and content is located in the manner by which content is to be understood. Content within the model merely demarcates what is conveyed, not what its import is or who or which groups are addressed (interpellated) or marginalized. Content is the information, the data which the meme conveys. Stance is the deliberation on how that content should be (ideally) understood and which (imagined) audiences are addressed and which are ignored, marginalized, etc. With image-based (or simply, non-video) memes, it may be helpful to start not with content or stance but rather with form, then follow with the analysis with the knowledge proffered by a merging of the content and stance dimensions.

Applying the Elaboration of Shifman's Model to Image-Based Memes

As an applied example, I will examine the *Pompeii Victim* meme, in which an archaeological discovery led to the pervasiveness of dark humor on social media, according to my elaboration of Shifman's model. In May 2018, Italian archaeologists announced the startling discovery of an intact skeleton of a man, believed to have died in his 30s, who fled the eruption of Mount Vesuvius which entombed the city of Pompeii in ash in 79 CE (Joseph, 2018). The man was believed to have suffered from a bone infection which hampered his gait during his attempted escape and making him a likely victim for his fate: despite surviving the initial explosions of Vesuvius' eruptions, a small boulder crushed his upper body, causing instant death.

Introduce the Internet

Shortly after the announcement was made, Twitter users tweeted and Facebook users posted remixed images of the boulder-crushed-skeleton to advance notions of dark humor, distanced irony, and displaced malaise. In terms of form, users simply took the image and added text, making it a version of an image-macro meme. In its conveyance of ideas and ideology, the boulder represents some form of obstacle, both metaphorically and literally (for the victim), and the victim represents the target of the obstacle. Stance provides a clear glimpse into how users deploy semiotic choices to advance a changed meaning, building on what Shifman (2013) calls the decision "to imitate a certain position that they find appealing or use an utterly different discursive orientation" (p. 367). Semiotically, users employ the meme to convey dark humor representative of some aspect of modern society or a current event. The boulder, with its lethal power, forces the victim, dead for over 2,000 years, to live again, memetically, only to be killed recursively in the force of the meme's function (also) as a joke. In each instance of the meme's iterations, something in the external world is critiqued, and the function of the boulder is to represent the weight of the worthiness of the critique.

One version in particular criticizes s*ocial media* as deterministically crushing and killing *civil discourse*. Intertextually, the meme bridges the knowledge of the archaeological discovery with the semiotic function of remixing the meme for making new meaning according to ideological practice. In this instance, the nature of social media, with all its trappings and dark sides (Levinson, 2013, p. 161; Stephens-Davidowitz, 2017, p. 160), is positioned as an archetypal threatening force set to undermine individuals' abilities to engage in reasoned and civil debate and discourse. The same semiotic and intertextual function occurs in another version of the meme, however social media is replaced by the *relentless news cycle*. In both instances, the user-as-victim has already succumbed to the predetermined fate but is remixable depending on the intended message.

In terms of ideological practice, the suggestion in these examples is that some other external entity or force is acting against our wishes. This sentiment has social salience at least in part due to the challenges posed by the modern era, that is a resurgence in nationalism, nativism, etc. in the USA and Europe, uncertainty about potential war(s) with

Iran, North Korea, accusations of Russian political interference in other countries, among other issues. While these memes present a humorous effect, they inhere the visual argument that all is not well with a certain issue and, furthermore, '*I identify with the victim because the issue at hand is crushing me*'.

In closing, I have shown the analytical value of elaborating on Shifman's (2013) tripartite typology of memetic dimensions of content, form, and stance. My contribution adds to the model in terms of using stance and content more concretely with respect to semiotic and intertextual meaning-making in the expression of an ideological practice. In general, my suggestion is to dig deeply when analyzing internet memes and to attempt to ascertain the ideological implications of a given meme, in terms also of how its meaning is constructed and what it uses to *make sense* in an increasingly TLDR (too long, didn't read) world.

The following chapters offer guidance in the form of case studies which undergo a critical discourse analysis in the tradition of Fairclough (1995) given the assertion and evidence that internet memes augment human language much in the same way that different fonts impact meaning, the insertion of visuals, emoticons, emojis, etc. similarly function as an ancillary linguistic apparatus.

References

Aunger, R. (2002). *The electric meme: A new theory of how we think*. New York: The Free Press.

Blackmore, S. (2000). *The meme machine* (New ed.). Oxford: Oxford University Press.

Burman, J. (2012). The misunderstanding of memes: Biography of an unscientific object, 1976–1999. *Perspectives on Science, 20*(1), 75–104.

Dawkins, R. (1989). *The selfish gene* (New ed.). Oxford: Oxford University Press.

Dawkins, R. (2013). *Just for hits*. Retrieved from http://www.youtube.com/watch?v=GFn-ixX9edg

Eco, U. (1984). *Semiotics and the philosophy of language*. Hong Kong: Macmillan.

Fairclough, N. (1995). *Critical discourse analysis: The critical study of language*. London: Longman.

Finnegan, C. A. (2001). The naturalistic enthymeme and visual argument: Photographic representation in the "skull controversy". *Argumentation and Advocacy, 37*, 133–149.

Gabielkov, M., Ramachandran, A., Chaintreau, A., & Legout, A. (2016). Social clicks: What and who gets to read on Twitter? *Proceedings from Sigmetrics 2016 Conference*. Antibes Juan-Les-Pins, France. Retrieved from https://hal.inria.fr/hal-01281190/document

Goffman, E. (1974). *Frame analysis*. Cambridge, MA: Harvard University Press.

Hofstadter, D. (1983). Metamagical themas: Virus-like sentences and self-replicating structures. *Scientific American, 248*, 14–22.

Huntington, H. E. (2017). Pepper spray cop and the American dream: Using synecdoche and metaphor to unlock internet memes' visual political rhetoric. *Communication Studies, 67*(1), 77–93.

Jakobson, R. (1960). Closing statement: Linguistics and poetics. In T. Sebeok (Ed.), *Style in language* (pp. 350–377). Cambridge: MIT Press.

Jenkins, H. (2009, February 11). *If it doesn't spread, it's dead (part one): Media viruses and memes* [Web log post]. Retrieved from http://henryjenkins.org/2009/02/if_it_doesnt_spread_its_dead_p.html

Joseph, Y. (2018, May 30). He fled the ash that buried Pompeii, only to be crushed by a rock. *The New York Times.* Retrieved from https://www.nytimes.com/2018/05/30/world/europe/pompeii-skeleton-rock.html?smtyp=cur&smid=tw-nytimes

Kien, G. (2013). Media memes and prosumerist ethics: Notes toward a theoretical examination of memetic audience behavior. *Critical Studies? Critical Methodologies, 13*(6), 554–561. doi:10.1177/1532708613503785

Levinson, P. (2013). *New new media* (2nd ed.). New York: Penguin.

Milner, R. M. (2012). *The world made meme: Discourse and identity in participatory media* (PhD thesis). University of Kansas, Lawrence, KS. Retrieved from http://kuscholarworks.ku.edu/handle/1808/10256

Pearce, K. E., & Hajizada, A. (2014). No laughing matter: Humor as a means of dissent in the digital era: The case of authoritarian Azerbaijan. *Demokratizatsiya, 22*, 67–85. Retrieved from https://www.gwu.edu/~ieresgwu/assets/docs/demokratizatsiya%20archive/GWASHU_DEMO_22_1/B158221228502786/B158221228502786.pdf

Shifman, L. (2011). Anatomy of a YouTube meme. *New Media & Society, 14*(2), 187–203. doi:10.1177/1461444811412160

Shifman, L. (2013). Memes in a digital world: Reconciling with a conceptual troublemaker. *Journal of Computer-Mediated Communication, 18*, 362–377.

Shifman, L. (2014). *Memes in digital culture.* Cambridge: MIT Press.

Smith, V. J. (2007). Aristotle's classical enthymeme and the visual argument of the twenty-first century. *Argumentation and Advocacy, 43*(Winter & Spring), 114–123.

Stephens-Davidowitz, S. (2017). *Everybody lies: Big data and what the internet can tell us about who we really are.* New York: Harper Collins.

Varis, P., & Blommaert, J. (2015). Conviviality and collectives on social media: Virality, memes, and new social structures. *Multilingual Margins, 2*(1), 31–45.

Weng, L., Flammini, A., Vespignani, A., & Menczer, F. (2012) Competition among memes in a world with limited attention. *Scientific Reports, 2*(335), 120–138.

Wiggins, B. E. (2017). Navigating an immersive narratology: Fake news and the 2016 U.S. Presidential campaign. *International Journal of E-Politics, 8*(3), 16–33. doi:10.4018/IJEP.2017070101

Williams, R. (1981). *Culture.* London: Fontana.

2 The Discursive Power of Memes in Digital Culture

The main thrust of this chapter is to situate internet memes in terms of their supposed discursive power in digital culture. Further, as noted in Chapter 1, throughout this work memes are analyzed and discussed with respect to ideology, semiotics, and intertextuality. These three concepts are addressed after a brief overview of discourse.

The phrase *discursive power* inheres an agency possessing the capacity to do something, that is, to engage in the constituting and reconstituting of social relations in online spaces. However, social relations are also constituted and reconstituted offline given the degree to which individuals remember, create, talk about, etc. internet memes (or any other related content, for that matter). This is also an early indication of the usefulness of Giddens' term *memory traces*, which assist in the agential enactment or performance of acts based on expected social interactions within a social system (discussed in greater detail in the following chapter).

To return to the phrase *discursive* power, one must ask what the power actually is and why or how is the power described as discursive. The location of the answer is *digital culture*, at least partially. The interrelationship shared between ideology, semiotics, and intertextuality enables both (1) a deeper and meaningful understanding of internet memes and (2) an opportunity to explore memes in a context where the discussion is conscious of the interrelationship and the implications which that nexus necessarily has on communication. It is important to define what is meant by *digital culture*.

Digital Culture

At the core of it, digital culture means the interaction between human and computer. The critical aspect to remember is that this is not a one-way interaction. Digital culture may commonly be assumed to mean using social media as the primary form of interacting with other human beings. This simple yet pervasive interaction implies so much more. You want to watch a speech of a political official, you can live stream it. You want to meet a friend at a café, you can use an app to track where your friend is, find a café, catch up on your messages, respond to emails, listen to a podcast or music, and tap into the local Wi-Fi. Selfies, hashtags, digital assistants, life hacks, sharing every moment with the screens we carry, wearable technologies, artificial intelligence, transhumanism, extreme and sophisticated personalization, the internet of things, etc. are all digital culture.

My treatment of *digital culture* is a variation of Jenkins' (2009) definition of *participatory culture* which he asserts has "relatively low barriers to artistic expression and civic engagement, strong support for creating and sharing one's creations, and some type of informal mentorship whereby what is known by the most experienced is passed along to novices" (p. 3). Absent from Jenkins' work, however, is an integrated approach to explaining that participatory culture is *not* a utopian plateau where all have equal access, entry, and impact. Consider the financial negotiations between a site such as YouTube or Instagram and its users who benefit from having a large following. A participatory culture where some are remunerated for their activities and others merely *participate* is at best an uneven and wildly optimistic view of online participatory communities of scale. To this I add that digital culture should not be viewed as a homologous gestalt, which I suspect is possible given Jenkins' rather vague and optimistic categories. Obviously, Jenkins is describing the process of dynamic interaction and cultural production which the internet and related technologies enable. However, we need a broad definition that clarifies the concept and de-emphasizes the shareability of digital items and elevates the relationship to discourse. The function of *digital culture* as a term acknowledges a departure from earlier forms of media largely dominated by print, radio, and television and a movement toward personalization, user-generated content, algorithmic news feeds, and a fear of missing out. These are obviously only a few aspects of digital culture as a concept, and the term *digital* alongside *culture* is important to reflect upon at least for what that association implies. Cultures are lived; the digital is programmed. A merging of the two represents a technological achievement tantamount to praise and concern. However, older technologies such as television invited concern and critical reception much in the same way considering the current case with the internet and its permutations.

Older Fears and New Rationalities

Cultural theorist Raymond Williams (1975) makes note of the ways in which television had changed the world since its inception as a mass medium in the twentieth century in his book *Television: Technology and Cultural Form*. In it, he lists a series of statements that attest to the fantastic ways in which television is molding the world. Indeed, his list compares quite well with the assumptions about how the internet is changing the world, society, etc. One such example that: "[t]elevision was invented as the result of scientific and technical research. Its inherent properties as an electronic medium altered our basic perceptions of reality, and thence our relations with each other and with the world" (Williams, 1975, p. 11). However, as Miller (2011) astutely notes, the internet is perhaps better poised to affect social relations in terms of the technologies used to enhance communication, information accessing, and more. The point is that with regard to digital culture, we need not focus on the internet alone. Clearly, *digital* encompasses mobile technologies, computer-based systems, radio, television, film, etc. With respect to the way I use the term in this book, *digital culture* is perhaps best viewed as a kind of bridge between online and offline worlds.

Accordingly, *digital culture* is a space that links online and offline interactions related to the internet and its affordances. As a space it is occupied; it is impossible for *digital culture* to exist and simultaneously not be occupied. In other words, it necessitates human agents for the continued recursive formation and reification of itself in order to exist and to have an influence on how we engage in expressing ourselves, responding to expressions, etc. Within this space discourses emerge as a consequence of human interaction. With the added detail of the digital, human communication is enhanced but also constrained by the composition of a given discourse. One such discourse is the discourse of internet memes. Other discourses could be, for example, the discourse of cyberbullying or trolling, the discourse of emojis, the discourse of Twitter. What they share is an inhibitive force, one that at once is creative and also constraining, given the expectations that *certain things should mean certain things and only those things.*

The Power of Discourse

To speak of discourse is to acknowledge locational subjective spaces constituted by a topical alignment of meaning. By implication, a discourse emphasizes uniformity of ideational constructs to allow for the continuation of itself. The French linguist Benveniste (1966, in Macey, 2000) offered that a discourse is defined by illocution, intent, and to some degree, a desire among human beings to be persuasive. This linguistic articulation of discourse is helpful as it provides a glimpse into the limits of what and how linguistics can assist in defining discourse. While linguistics is chiefly interested in the study of language and its syntactic, historical, neurological, etc. structure, critical theory is necessary to address the existence of discourses and their influence on human beings. Accordingly, the work of Michel Foucault is particularly helpful in addressing the *power* of discourse.

A discourse, be it the discourse of 19th century British literature, the discourse of comic books, or the discourse of *Star Trek*, is comprised of a set of possible utterances and other forms of expression which direct and constrain what human agents can understand and what meanings can be articulated concerning a particular field of knowledge or subject matter. Foucault (1989) emphasizes the duality of social relations in his articulation of discourses as consisting of "practices that systematically form the object of which they speak", otherwise conceptualized as discursive formations (p. 49). With this view of discourse, human beings construct reality not in terms of the actual physical world but the world of social relations. Meaning is created and negotiated by human agential action.

However, discourses are liberating as well as constraining. We can say a discourse is liberating in that it allows for expression to take place, but this expression is invariably constrained by the limits afforded by language and semiotics. This view of discourse is extended by Herbert Marcuse, who wrote in *One-Dimensional Man* (1964) that due to the consumer-driven aspect of capitalism and the need for the continual production and consumption of items, services, etc., discourse itself has become flattened. In other words, in order to operate within a social system, it is required to adhere to specific forms of expression (to avoid certain words or phrases, to use language in such a way to constrain meaning, to adapt to the dominant social order, etc.) and while those expressions may denote a critical or liberating response, they are still trapped within the social system in which they are uttered.

Discourse as Ideology

Discourse is perhaps best viewed as a synonym for ideology. A system of knowledge and behaviors which directs communication also inhibits it, constrains what is possible and delineates what is marginal. This is what we should understand by the term discourse as it is used in this work. With respect to the title of this work, *the discourse of memes* is best understood, specifically, as *the discursive power of digital culture* which I explicitly define conceptually as constituting ideology, semiotics, and intertextuality. Thus, these words are not randomly selected. Their purpose is to highlight the role of internet memes in digital culture in terms of discourse, as has been discussed above.

The language used to discuss a given discourse is entangled with meaning and sets of expectations of certain forms of meaning, constraint, redirection, etc. In order for individuals to interact with one another in a social system (or systems), it is simply required that specific known behaviors and communicative strategies be maintained, and their maintenance communicates this process to others so that the system is preserved.

With internet memes, we have an opportunity to view discourse(s) in action. At a minimum, any given internet meme inheres ideological practice, especially if the meme expresses a view that is critical (even in an overtly humorous way) of the political, social, economic, cultural, etc. spheres. Additionally, in order for the ideology to be understood, certain semiotic constructions must be achieved for meaning to be consolidated in an enthymemetic process that occurs between an individual or groups of individuals and a given internet meme. Further, intertextuality often aids in both processes, but is not essential. Within the course of this book, I write about ideology, semiotics, and intertextuality vis-à-vis internet memes. However, it is sufficient to compact these three subtitular terms into *memes as discourse*.

Ideology

As noted earlier, it is helpful to view discourse, as described and defined herein, as a tenable synonym for ideology. However, it is in the relationship between ideological formation and semiotic meaning-making that a conceptual distinction is made possible, and also, is essential to understand why I have parsed discourse down to these three constitutive categories. The chief distinction for the purposes of this discussion – both of the larger topic of internet memes as well as the terms *ideology* and *discourse* themselves – is that ideology, by itself, is all-encompassing, permeating every social interaction, saturating every thought and utterance, while discourse, again also a suitable synonym for ideology in general, is first and foremost defined by communication. While this may be obvious, I emphasize it here because I wish to draw attention to certain assumptions which may or may not be widely shared or understood. First, when I say that discourse is defined by communication, I do not negate what I previously discussed regarding discourse. Rather, I simply emphasize that discourse as communication is never accidental; it is always purposeful. This is an important point upon which to reflect. The purpose or intent may be guided by discursive formations emanating from a dominant social order, which clearly appears as a surrogate for ideology writ large. Yet, discourse as communication remains expressly purposeful, while ideology is ideational.

The reason for this intentional exploration of ideology as a concept is that it is somewhat maligned by competing meanings, similar to *culture* or *gender*, for example. Storey (2006) provides an excellent overview of different approaches to defining *ideology*. He explains that ideology is nothing more than "a systematic body of ideas articulated by a particular group of people" (Storey, 2006, p. 2). The primary emphasis here is on the ideational mode with ideology, thus also implying a communicative mode with discourses. This broad definition actually accomplishes something quite clever. By naming the collection of ideas, a *systematic body* and by describing the action undertaken by people who *sub*scribe to the group of ideas as *articulation*, the achievement of ideology appears to liberate a group, allowing or prescribing certain actions. However, those actions are already defined or at least we have some degree of rational expectation of what types of actions the *systematic body* is interested in producing, in allowing, etc.

A second definition emanates from classical Marxism and is concerned with the claim of *false consciousness* as the deterministic function of ideology. In this definition, ideology masks or conceals reality in such a way that what the average working person sees is merely presented as a version of reality, and one that solely serves the needs and requirements of dominant, powerful elites. It is not important what the individual believes or thinks about the dominant social order; however, it is critical that the individual follows orders, that is, to acquire and consume material possessions and to view themselves not as oppressed but as living their lives the way they want. Thus, '*they do not know what they are doing, but they do it anyway*' approaches a fine summary of this version of ideology. Also, it is important to note that the dominant, powerful elites do not view themselves as the oppressors; if anything, the elites are also '*just living their lives*' thereby also benefiting from the concealment of the true nature of reality.

A third definition of ideology describes it as conceptually similar to the second definition. Storey (2006) maintains that "texts always present an image of the world...with society structured around inequality, exploitation and oppression" (p. 3). He suggests that all texts are political; *text* is anything that can carry a message and that can be understood, analyzed, decoded, reacted to, disputed, etc., which is strikingly similar to the *sign* in semiotics, to be discussed in a subsequent section. Stuart Hall adds to this sentiment of ideology his treatment of popular culture. Basically, he views popular culture as a conduit for the production and dissemination of "collective social understandings", or discourses, whose purpose is the achievement of acceptance by a person or group. Hall refers to codes as the place from which signs emanate; the *sign* is a semiotic term that essentially demarcates a meeting point for signifier and signified; it forms the building blocks of any knowable (social) reality. Hall (1980) claims that codes "are the means by which power and ideology are made to signify in particular discourses" (p. 134). In order to get people to view the world you want them to see, they must acquiesce to your presentation.

Acquiescence is the result of viewing texts as signposts of ideology; in order to get people to accept your particular presentation of the world, it is crucial to speak to them in terms they will understand and accept. This is particularly helpful and relevant to (current) discussions of *fake news*. With this seemingly problematic term, it is important to unpack its full meaning, which I view as a bifurcation emanating from assumptions about sources of truth in an increasingly mediated environment. I have noted elsewhere that,

[i]n terms of conceptual orientation, fake news refers to news stories which are not based on objective or verifiable fact, evidence, testimony, etc., whereas claims that real news stories or professional news companies such as The New York Times or CNN embody fake news represents an existential challenge to their function in society. Disagreement with a fact-based news report based on personal opinion now appears to be justification for applying the moniker fake news whenever it seems appropriate.

(Wiggins, 2017a, p. 17)

The relationship between the Storey's (2006) third definition of *ideology* and *fake news* has to do with a disavowal of evidence-based argument, discussion, and debate and the tendency to accuse the other of a misdeed when presented with anything that could challenge one's ideological practice. In the presentation of texts as representations of the world, if the purpose is to *re-present* some attribute of the world or system we inhabit, this is also a manufactured construction. Even when we report on a real-world event, we must deliberate within the confines of language, connotation, image referents, etc. to construct the world through the texts presented to the viewer, spectator, individual, etc. I explore this in greater detail in Chapter 6 where I introduce my conceptualization of *media narrative* and its relevance to internet memes.

To return to defining ideology with respect to internet memes, a fourth definition highlights the work of French philosopher, Roland Barthes. Specifically, Barthes uses the term *myth* for what might normally signify *ideology*. Barthes equates myth with ideology given his emphasis on the connotative power of the text-image relationship. The purpose of ideology is "to make universal and legitimate what is partial and particular" (Storey, 2006, p. 3). Barthes (1977) states that

[m]yth does not deny things, on the contrary, its function is to talk about them; simply, it purifies them, it makes them innocent, it gives them a clarity which is not that of an explanation but that of a statement of fact.

(p. 301)

Here, Barthes refers to the ways myth is used to talk about a subject but only so far as to capture the desired content, omitting that which could delegitimize the argument and presume it all to be equal to fact.

In language, we make distinctions between perceived universals alongside implied marginality. For example, the phrases *woman doctor, African American basketball player, transgender politician, vegan boyfriend,* etc. all at once are expressly liberated by the act of demarcating "other" as opposed to hiding or concealing it while simultaneously implying a possible deviant relationship against an assumed *normal* or *superior* other. This process is present in internet memes which seek to challenge or critique, for example, a political opponent. For example, the *Turning Point USA* political action committee actively deploys image macro memes that lambaste socialism and equates it with the vanguard of uninformed, opinionated perspectives of communism. Other themes include a general distrust of big government, appeals to tradition, and suggesting that racism is not real but exists as an insult against white people by black people. Figure 2.1 includes a representative example.

This image is a classic example of using a strawman argumentative approach in critique of individuals with a politically left lean. Hashtags that often accompany such posts are #socialismkills or #communismkills. It is not my purpose to defend Marx or take a political position, but the image should demonstrate how memes can recast the *other* in a way that appeals to a particular ideological practice. Even if you were to agree with the meme, I would encourage you to do a little bit of research and investigate *beyond* the meme. It is worthwhile to note the high number of reactions (over 14,000, of these 9,300 are likes; 2,600 angry faces; 925 wow faces; 789 crying faces; 328 laughing faces; 68 hearts/love) and shares (over 18,000) compared with the relatively low number of comments (1,135). This suggests it is more important and alluring to react to the meme, reifying one's identity and ideology, as well as it is to use the meme as a discursive unit by sharing it within one's network. It would be interesting to know how many of the people who

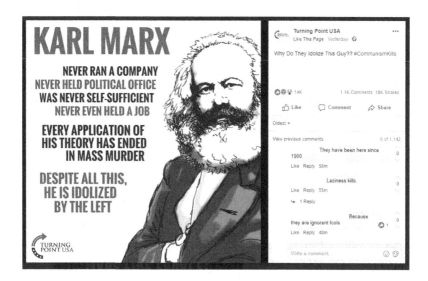

Figure 2.1 Turning Point USA: Remixing Karl Marx.

reacted to it in a specific way also shared it, and whether a thematically consonant comment was made as well.

In many other related *Turning Point USA* memes, the *text* only presents what it is comfortable with, however the source of the anxiety is also revealed but normally uses one or many logical fallacies. Following this example, ideology allows the discussion of *other* and here the group *Turning Point USA* positions wealth inequality as emblematic of the other. The meme presents simultaneously the preferred ideological practice as well as the vocabulary to be used by the (imagined) audience it addresses and the out-group, the marginal perspectives that should be challenged, mocked, etc. through the deployment of the meme. In other words, myth is a two-way street: whether you agree or disagree you are still ensconced within ideology.

Another definition of ideology comes from Louis Althusser (2006) who described ideology as a set of beliefs and practices which serve to connect a person to the world and vice versa. Individuals express themselves according to a particular worldview regardless of how sophisticated or base it may be. Further, expression of this worldview is tethered to actions largely determined by sets of beliefs, values, and assumptions that link us to the world or social system, etc.

Althusser, like Zizek, draws implicitly on Lacanian psychoanalytic theory to articulate ideology. Eagleton (2008) provides an excellent reading of Althusser in which he writes, in the first person that:

> It is as though society were not just an impersonal structure to me, but a 'subject' which 'addresses' me personally – which recognizes me, tells me that I am valued, and so makes me by that very act of recognition into a free, autonomous subject. I come to feel, not exactly as though the world exists for me alone, but as though it is significantly 'centered' on me, and I in turn am significantly 'centered' on it. Ideology…is the very medium in which I 'live out' my relation to society, the realm of signs and social practices which binds me to the social structures and lends me a sense of coherent purpose and identity.
>
> (Eagleton, 2014, p. 149)

Storey explains further that "certain rituals and customs have the effect of binding us to the social order". Rather cynically but appropriately, Storey (2006, p. 4) uses the example of a "seaside holiday or the celebration of Christmas" as examples of how individuals may escape the demands of the given social order, but the expectation is that they must inevitably return to the social order. For Althusser, the function of *ideology* is not a mask that conceals reality, nor is it simply an arrangement of textual representation of the world for compliance gaining and agreement with a set of ideas-as-facts. Rather, and perhaps more darkly, the function is to reproduce the social conditions such that the conditions required for the continuation of capitalism (or any socio-economic system) must be ever maintained and iteratively and recursively reproduced, in order to guarantee the persistence of the same social system.

Althusser claims that in ideology, an individual is interpellated (or hailed, addressed) by society and the individual's ensuing actions, thoughts, behaviors, etc. are not necessarily guided or determined by ideology but rather by the individual subject who engages and interacts with other subjects in a social system. This is in the sense that *'I'm living my life'* or *'This is who I am'*, etc. where what is thought of as normal or deviant, possible or impossible (in terms of social relations), etc. is constrained and defined by the ideological practice(s) which interpellates an individual subject.

To this I add Zizek's extension of Althusser's work drawn heavily on Lacanian psychoanalysis, Marxist dialectic, and the work of Deleuze and Guattari. Zizek (2009) rejects the notion of false consciousness and elevates the Althusserian notion of interpellation of the subject as an object of desire. Zizek claims that desire is (always already) that which drives agents to engage with others within the social system, itself mired in capitalist commodification and fetishization of cultural products whose connection to agents define the nature of social relations. For Zizek, the ultimate horror of desire is for the desire to be completely fulfilled.

Ideology and Internet Memes

My use of the term *ideology* in this work primarily centers on Barthes and Hall as well as Althusser and Zizek. While I have reviewed several views on ideology, my intention is to connect internet memes with ideological practice. Memes are produced to mean something and in the process of interpretation and comprehension, this actually becomes a process of ideological formation *indicative* of an ideological practice.

I primarily refer to those memes which have as their subject matter some form of critique of a social, cultural, political, economic, and/or related phenomena. With the phrase *ideological practice,* I emphasize the Althusserian and Zizekian views comingled with the aspect that it is conducted, acted upon, produced, etc. through human agential interactions with the social system. This practice emanates, neutrally, from the interaction between human agents and the social system to form the essence of what Giddens (1984) calls the *duality of structure*, or more succinctly, structuration. I elaborate in greater detail the relationship between structuration and internet memes in the following chapter. However, it is sufficient at this point to underscore the function of ideology in social interactions as a liberating and also a constraining force, not dissimilar to discourse, as noted above.

Internet memes as a subject of study are incredibly visual given the propensity for memes to rely on images for the dissemination of a particular message. Accordingly, a discussion of the production (or manufacture) of meaning visually and verbally must be carried out within the frame of semiotics. The rationale for this is precisely because of the relationship between ideological practice and the construction of meaning.

Semiotics

Any discussion or reference to ideology can become loaded with potential misunderstandings or associations with political philosophies and related schools of thought. For my treatment of internet memes, it is essential that I bridge ideology with semiotics. Why is this the case? If we understand ideology – again similar to discourse – as a constraining yet also liberating function of agential interaction in a social system, it is necessary to understand how meaning is produced in such a process. My analysis and later contextualized discussions of internet memes in practice benefits from several perspectives on semiotics.

Semiotics as a discipline emerged from the work of Ferdinand de Saussure and Charles Sanders Peirce and is primarily concerned with how meaning is constructed in ideas as well as objects and persons. Specifically, semiotics is a theoretical approach to develop a science of signs, or perhaps more appropriately, to develop a way to study how signs operate, manifest, and expressed in social relations.

However, it was Roland Barthes who extended the field of semiotics to include units of signification unique to a given discourse. His work expands semiotics to include also other sign-systems such as images, nonverbal communication, and even sounds. Umberto Eco perhaps contributed most significantly to the field of semiotics by his elaboration of the sign and the development of interpretative semiotics.

Central to semiotics is the sign. For Eco, the sign is akin to a gesture or indication of meaning and is "produced with *the intention of* communication, that is, in order to transmit one's representation or inner state to another being" (1984, p. 16). Essentially, Eco builds on the work of Peirce, Saussure, Jakobson, Greimas, Hjelmslev, and others to suggest that the utility of the sign resides in its function to transmit information, to say or to indicate a thing that is knowable. Interestingly, Blommaert (2015) asserts that internet memes (though he calls them *viral memes*) should be understood as identical to the semiotic sign, a view also emphasized by Cannizzaro (2016). Blommaert (2015) emphasizes that "the sign is deployed to *do different things* in the communicative environment where it is deployed. Its effects will depend on how the interlocutors understand this function" (p. 16). However, his emphasis lies more on the virality of memes-as-signs than on the cultural experience and the capacity for memes to convey nuances of ideological practice.

A distinction must be made between natural signs and artificial or conventional signs. The former emanates from the natural world, whereas the latter is produced for the purpose of signification, of meaning-making. Signs, however, must not be confused with codes, or language systems. For Eco (1984), a code is a formative series of rules which permits or enables the process of attributing signification to a sign. Some disagreement exists as to what the sign, code, etc. is or is not. For example, what Barthes (1977) includes as an expansion of semiotics to include other sign-systems such as images or nonverbal communication is also what Jakobson (1960) defines as codes. Regardless of internal disagreement, the purpose of applying semiotics to the study of internet memes has to do with the *function* of meaning and how it is constructed. One particularly helpful perspective which relates to meaning but also to channels, or media, which transmit meaning comes from an individual not usually associated with semiotics.

Marshall McLuhan, communications theorist, proposed rather succinctly in the phrase "the medium is the message", that the communication channels we select for verbal as well as visual expressions necessarily impact the message. In the first case, this phrase suggests that human beings use *media* rather broadly, and here we must quickly remind ourselves that this word means channels of communication (email, newspaper, tweets, video games, movie posters, advertising, etc.) and not news media. In other words, human beings use technologies of mass communication to reach outwardly both cognitively and socially. However, a second meaning of this phrase more closely pertains to semiotics, especially semiotics of mediated forms of communication in online spaces such as memes. Perhaps what is most elusive, but also provocative, about *the medium is the message* is that "the dominant media used to communicate in a society in a specific historical epoch affect the content of the messages communicated" (Danesi, 2010, p. 138). The pervasiveness of internet memes is not a simple permutation of Dawkins' original idea of the *meme* but rather a symptom of the interaction between human beings and social systems afforded by digital culture. I claim that internet memes represent an elaboration of McLuhan's (1994) *message*, and that they are a genre of communication consonant with the technological affordances and quiddities of the internet (Wiggins & Bowers, 2014).

Semiotics and Internet Memes

In a sense, we can view internet memes as a real-world representation of the more abstract claims associated with Derrida's view that signs refer to other signs which refer still to other signs. Additionally, we can view memes as representative of a claim associated with the Frankfurt School and later again with Baudrillard. Namely, a culture which is so saturated with media usage recursively produces and reproduces texts for (instant) consumption. Despite the potential for rapid consumption and production, internet memes persist. They possess the potential to permeate all forms of discourse precisely due to the inherent affordances of digital culture and the use of online forms of communication.

Internet memes contain within them a semiotic meaning which is itself tethered to an ideological practice. Of course, not all memes are heavily rich in ideology, such as the rather old *Doge* meme. However, even the *Doge* meme can be remixed to convey a semiotic message consonant with a particular ideology. The preponderance of internet memes online and covering a range of topics from the mundane and the quotidian, to the sublime, controversial, and/or provocative is an outcome of the second reading of McLuhan's *the medium is the message*: online communication structures and the availability of rapid access to people and information means a massive demand on attention. The internet meme is, therefore, a perfectly truncated genre of communication for online audiences, both real and imagined.

But what of the relationship between semiotics and ideology? Why should we view them as complementary to each other? Hodge (2017) argues that ideology as a concept is vital "to socially-oriented semiotics because it identifies a unitary object that incorporates complex sets of meanings with the social agents and processes that produced them". He builds on the work of others including Russian linguist Valentin Voloshinov who asserted the representational facet of any ideological system as dependent upon signs and symbols in order to convey meaning. In *Marxism and the philosophy of language*, Voloshinov (1973) argues that "[w]ithout signs there is no ideology...[e]verything ideological possesses semiotic value" (p. 9). Drawing also on Gramsci (hegemony) and Althusser (ideology; interpellation), Hodge and Kress (1988) emphasize the role of *contradiction* as a constitutive element crucial to any ideological perspective and propose the following definition of,

> ideological complexes, [which exist as] a functionally related set of contradictory versions of the world, coercively imposed by one social group on another on behalf of its distinctive interests, or subversively offered by another social group in attempts at resistance in its own interests.
>
> (p. 3)

The function of ideology is to constrain behavior, direct it in ways preferred by the dominant mode or group. It is a view of society rooted in the argument that while ideology is a lived experience, it also embraces the imagined relationships individuals have to their real-life conditions, experiences, etc. Further, and following Althusser (2006), ideology is much more effective to maintain ruling power than physical force.

If individuals act according to beliefs which conform to their worldview and hold a conscious or semi-conscious disagreement with another worldview, this is accomplished (using codes, or rules and symbols for communicating as noted earlier). Either explicitly or implicitly, certain specific utterances or expressions become extensions of their behavior, itself defined by ideological practice. In other words, in the act of verbal or textual expression, an individual makes certain semiotic choices in the agreement or disagreement with the message in an internet meme. The sharing, liking, commenting upon, curating, etc. of the meme also helps to foment ideological practice. Throughout this work, I refer to processes of meaning-making and how the selection of certain intertextual references also guides the role of semiotic construction in internet memes. The final aspect of the discursive power of memes in digital culture is intertextuality and is discussed in the following section.

Intertextuality

It is important to note the origin of the term *intertextual*. Kristeva (1980) introduced intertextuality in order to bridge Saussurean semiotics (specifically, in terms of how signs attain meaning within the structure of a given text) with Bakhtin's dialogism (which explained that an ongoing dialogue persists in relation to other works of literature and other authors). For Kristeva, intertextuality means that a given text does not exist as an independent or closed unit or system.

An internet meme cannot exist without referring to something other than the subject matter it contains. For example, the *Twilight Zone Trump* meme demonstrates this, and without the need for verbal text. In the meme, a scene from an episode of *The Twilight Zone* depicts a troubled man seated in the cabin of an airplane looking desperately toward the viewer in reaction to a supposed gremlin monster looking into the plane from the outside. Simply by replacing the image of monster and inserting an ideologically motivated choice, in one such case President Donald Trump, an intertextual relationship is created (Wiggins, 2017b). Within this intertextual relationship, however, exists ideological practice constructed in part through deliberate semiotic choices in the interest of making meaning, and perhaps most importantly, making certain that the constructed meaning be as understandable as possible, whether directed at mass or discrete audiences.

Intertextuality and Internet Memes

Previous scholarship linking discussions of internet memes with intertextuality tended to emphasize the more obvious examples of intertextual messages in memes. For example, Shifman (2014) cites intertextuality as "additional layers of meaning, associated with a text such as *Star*

*Wars...*add[ing] complexity and ambiguity to the message" (p. 150). However, a text such as *Star Wars* is itself intertextual. To explain this point briefly, *Star Wars* is a fine example of remix – taking of available content and essentially repackaging it in such a way to appear new for further consumption.

George Lucas purposefully employed Joseph Campbell's monomyth, or the hero's journey, in his development of the main story behind *Star Wars* (Kaminski, 2008). Additionally, Lucas cited the samurai films of Japanese director Akira Kurasowa in his presentation of Jedi knights fighting with light sabers (Kaminski, 2008, p. 46). *Star Wars* is itself intertextual as its filmic development is expansive such that it can refer to itself, to its own canonicity in the context of its own original films as compared with the prequels as well as with newer films since Disney's acquisition, not to mention the various animated and print-based iterations of the *Star Wars*.

The point here is that intertextuality should not be thought of as mere associations with other texts, for the singular purpose of adding meaning. Rather, intertextuality is purposeful, unavoidable, and ubiquitous. It is less helpful to think of individual texts referring to other texts in the process of making meaning as *intertextual*. Instead all texts are *intertexts*: references to other content, citations to previous work, allusions, parody, pastiche, etc. permeate all texts, and this is especially relevant and applicable to internet memes as a genre of online communication.

In the following chapter, the work of Anthony Giddens, specifically structuration, is employed to analyze a genre development of internet memes. At certain points throughout this work, I deviate from my own rather rigid genre development of internet memes in order to embrace a larger, more social media-centric perspective of memes in modern culture.

References

Althusser, L. (2006). Ideology and ideological state apparatuses (Notes toward an investigation). In M. G. Durham & D. M. Kellner (Eds.), *Media and cultural studies: Keyworks* (pp. 79–87). Malden, MA: Wiley-Blackwell.

Barthes, R. (1977). *Image-music-text*. London: Fontana.

Benveniste, E. (1966). *Problems of general linguistics* (M. E. Meek, Trans.). Miami: Miami University Press.

Blommaert, J. (2015). Meaning as a nonlinear effect: The birth of cool. In T. Lillis (Ed.), *Theory in applied linguistics research: Critical approaches to production, performance, and participation. AILA Review* (Vol. 28, pp. 7–27). John Benjamins Publishing Company.

Cannizzaro, S. (2016). Internet memes as internet signs: A semiotic view of digital culture. *Sign Systems Studies*, 44(4), 562–586.

Danesi, M. (2010). Semiotics of media and culture. In P. Cobley (Ed.), *The Routledge companion to semiotics* (pp. 135–149). New York: Routledge.

Eagleton, T. (2008). *Literary theory: An introduction* (Anniversary ed.). Minneapolis, MN: University of Minneapolis Press.

Eco, U. (1984). *Semiotics and the philosophy of language*. Hong Kong: Macmillan.

Foucault, M. (1989). *The archaeology of knowledge*. London: Routledge.

Giddens, A. (1984). *The constitution of society: Outline of the theory of structure*. Berkeley: University of California Press.

Hall, S. (1980). Encoding/decoding. In S. Hall, D. Hobson, A. Love, & P. Willis (Eds.), *Culture, media, language* (pp. 128–138). London: Hutchinson.

Hodge, R. (2017). Ideology. *Semiotics Encyclopedia Online*. Retrieved from https://semioticon.com/seo/I/ideology.html#

Hodge, R., & Kress, G. (1988). *Social semiotics*. Cambridge: Polity Press.

Jakobson, R. (1960). Closing statement: Linguistics and poetics. In T. Sebeok (Ed.), *Style in language* (pp. 350–377). Cambridge: MIT Press.

Jenkins, H. (2009). *Confronting the challenges of participatory culture: Media education for the 21st century*. Cambridge: The MIT Press.

Kaminski, M. (2008). *The secret history of Star Wars: The art of storytelling and the making of a modern epic*. Kingston, ON: Legacy Books. Retrieved from http://www.legacybookspress.com/Books/The%20Secret%20History%20of%20Star%20Wars%20-%20Free%20Sample.pdf

Kristeva, J. (1980). *Word, dialogue, and novel. Desire in language: A semiotic approach to literature and art* (T. Gora et al., Trans.). New York: Columbia University Press (Original work published 1977).

Macey, D. (2000). *Dictionary of critical theory*. London: Penguin Books.

Marcuse, H. (1964). *One-dimensional man*. London: Routledge & Kegan Paul.

McLuhan, M. (1994). *Understanding media* (Reprint ed.). Cambridge: MIT Press.

Miller, V. (2011). *Understanding digital culture*. Thousand Oaks, CA: Sage.

Shifman, L. (2014). *Memes in digital culture*. Cambridge: MIT Press.

Storey, J. (2006). *Cultural theory and popular culture* (4th ed.). Harlow: Pearson.

Voloshinov, V. (1973). *Marxism and the philosophy of language* (L. Matejka & I. R. Titunik, Trans.). New York: Seminar Press. (Original work published 1930).

Wiggins, B. E. (2017a). Navigating an immersive narratology: Fake news and the 2016 U.S. Presidential campaign. *International Journal of E-Politics, 8*(3), 16–33. doi:10.4018/IJEP.2017070101

Wiggins, B. E. (2017b). Digital dispatches from the 2016 US election: Popular culture, intertextuality and media power. *International Journal of Media & Cultural Politics, 13*(1–2), 197–205.

Wiggins, B. E., & Bowers, G. B. (2014). Memes as genre: A structurational analysis of the memescape. *New Media & Society, 17*(11), 1886–1906. doi:10.1177/1461444814535194

Williams, R. (1975). *Television: Technology and cultural form*. New York: Schocken Books.

Zizek, S. (2009). *The sublime object of ideology* (2nd ed.). London: Verso.

3 Memes as Genre[1]

In 1735, French artist Joseph Ducreux was born. Known for his portraits, Ducreux was made a baron and appointed first painter to Queen Marie Antoinette. In 1793, Ducreux finished his self-portrait Portrait de l'artiste sous les traits d'un moqueur (Self-portrait of the artist in the guise of a mockingbird). The portrait shows Ducreux, a French aristocrat dressed in a brown coat and black hat, smugly grinning, and pointing at the viewer (as shown in Figure 3.1).

Figure 3.1 Self-Portrait, ca. 1793 Joseph Ducreux.

Fast forward nearly 300 years to find Ducreux's painting on Reddit and Facebook pages as an image macro with one major alteration (an image macro is understood within popular culture as an image with captioned text). The portrait now included popular rap lyrics – lyrics which were altered to fit a more archaic form of speech. For instance, overlaid on top of the portrait are the words, "Gentlemen, I inquire who hath released the hounds?" which is a transformation of the popular lyrics, "Who let the dogs out?" Since its first appearance as an image macro in 2009 (Knowyourmeme.com, 2013a), hundreds of these transformations have occurred and have been distributed through social media (see Figure 3.2 for an example). Moreover, since its original occurrence, it has further mutated. In 2011, the Ducreux portrait now included a variation with actor Steve Buscemi's face added into the portrait (see Figure 3.3), with archaic interpretations of movie lines from *The Big Lebowski*, a film in which Buscemi acted.

Figure 3.2 Image Macro Meme of Ducreux's Self-Portrait.

Figure 3.3 Remixing Ducreaux: Steve Buscemi's face from The Big Lebowski.

The Ducreux image macro epitomizes the complex emergence, development, and transformation of memes. Fundamental to the meme's evolution is its movement from a simple stand-alone artifact to that of a full-fledged genre. It is a genre with its own set of rules and conventions, which emanate from postmodern conceptions of representation and replication and the obfuscation of the consumer/producer binary which is manifest in the practices of digital culture.

In what follows, a genre development of internet memes reveals a process underscored by transformation and dissemination. The aim in this chapter is to describe that the transformation of a singular iteration of an artifact can emerge as a full-fledged genre. Using Anthony Giddens' structuration theory, I analyze two memes – *The Most Interesting Man in the World* and *Distracted Boyfriend* – by placing them into the current media landscape and tracing their development as a genre.

Artifacts of Digital Culture

Internet memes exist as artifacts of participatory digital culture. Viewing memes as artifacts is helpful for three reasons. First, memes as artifacts possess virtual physicality meaning that internet memes are cognitive as well as digital. Virtual physicality is a seemingly contradictory term, yet it reveals that memes as artifacts exist in the human mind as well as in the digital environment. The recursive production, consumption, and reproduction of memes evince their importance and underscore their virtual physicality in participatory digital culture. Second, memes as artifacts highlight their social and cultural role on the new media landscape. Whereas a cultural artifact offers information about the culture that creates and uses it (Watts, 1981), a social artifact informs us about the social behavior of those individuals or groups which produce it (Wartofsky, 1979). Memes as artifacts possess both cultural and social attributes as they are produced, reproduced, and transformed to reconstitute the social system. In practical terms, the memetic social system is reconstituted when members of participatory digital culture use rules and resources of meme creation in the reproduction of further iterations of a given meme. In other words, the social system knows how to create a meme and that the creation or reproduction of memes may motivate the continued production of a given meme for an unknown period of time. Third, seeing memes as artifacts underscores the purposeful production and consumption among members of participatory digital culture. These three reasons (virtual physicality, social and cultural connection, and purposeful production and consumption) accentuate the meme as artifact but also relate directly to the duality of structure (Giddens, 1984), which implies an interaction between agent and social system. Before extending that discussion, it is prudent to deliberate on what constitutes a genre and how this relates to internet memes. Following my treatment of memes as genre, I analyze an image and video-based meme by drawing on structuration theory of Giddens (1984).

Genre

Unlike the traditional conception of genre, as a text (or utterance) of repeated forms and literary moves, genres are activities that guide and alter the dynamics of human culture. In this sense, a meme, viewed as a genre, is not simply a formula followed by humans to communicate, but represents a complex system of social motivations and cultural activity that is both a result of communication and impetus for that communication. Genres, therefore, are central to understanding culture. Bazerman and Russell (2003) suggest that genres are essentially "[h]uman-produced artifacts such as utterances or texts, or shovels or symphonies" and that we should not view such artifacts as *objects* per se but instead our focus should be on the "activities that give rise and use to them" (p. 1).

Kamberlis (1995, p. 141) notes that genres, or more precisely, the ways in which people employ genres for making utterances, meaning, etc., necessarily involves formal elements, thematic content, and discursive practice. With respect to genres as a means for understanding culture, Miller (1984, p. 165) suggests that genres function as an index to cultural patterns. It is interesting here to consider the term *index* as compared to Hall's notion of *codes* within discursive and/or ideological practices of meaning making, where the ability to produce meaning is at once emancipatory and constraining. To elaborate further on my own deliberation of culture and discourse from the previous chapter, to posit that culture is a lived experience means that people must use tools, such as genres, to make sense of the structure they inhabit, but also in specific and often formal if not also restrictive or deterministic ways. This is not to suggest that genres are fixed and immutable.

Kamberlis (1995, p. 140) reminds us that "as changes in genre occur, changes in ideologies and practices occur as well". However, as a means for expressing views within a culture, a genre must also inhere some degree of stability in order for meaning to be produced and understood. Kamberlis recalls Todorov in this regard to claim that

> [i]n a given society, the recurrence of certain discursive properties is institutionalized, and individual texts are produced and perceived in relation to the norm, constituted by that codification. A genre, whether literary or not, is nothing other than the codification of discursive properties.
>
> (Todorov, 1990, pp. 17–18, in Kamberlis, 1995, p. 124)

Further, by viewing memes as a genre of communication, they become objectified, something to be studied, evaluated, and the ideological practice they exhibit equally becomes to be deconstructed. Doing so situates our gaze on the activities, beliefs, assumptions, etc. that precipitated the memes and their spread.

Toward a Genre Development of Memes: Structuration Theory

Giddens' structuration theory has been used to analyze group communication (Poole, Seibold, & McPhee, 1996; Waldeck, Shepard, Teitelbaum, Farrar, & Seibold, 2002), e-commerce (Pavlou & Majchrzak, 2002), public relations (Falkheimer, 2009), and technology (Orlikowski, 1992, 2000). It was modified into adaptive structuration theory by DeSanctis and Poole (1994). It has also received criticism by Archer (1995) who regarded Giddens' insistence that agency and structure exist as a duality to be objectionable. Stones (2005) sought to reconfigure core structuration concepts such as agency and structure.

Structuration theory is built on the theoretical foundation of Norbert Elias, Pierre Bourdieu, Erving Goffman, and other sociological theorists such as Durkheim (Giddens, 1979, 1984). It was a critical response to the sociology of Parsons' (1951) actor-system theory outlined in *The Social System* which argued that norms generate structure and limit or constrain the ability of agency for change. Giddens, as Goffman (1956) before him, views language as a "self-enclosed reality [in which] meaning is bound up with practical activity in the real world" (Tucker, 1998, p. 79). Giddens argues that social action is linked directly to the creation of rules and practices which recursively constitute the structure wherein social action takes place. In structuration, agency and structure are separate only in terms of an analytical divide but are closer than the two-sided coin metaphor. Giddens views these as an interactive recursive relationship which involves rules, resources, social practices, and systems (Giddens, 1984).

Structures and Systems

Structuration theory seeks to understand interactions between individuals and the social structures in which they are active (Giddens, 1984, pp. 3–27; Orlikowski, 2000). For Giddens, structures are rules, resources, tasks, and norms. Rules and resources embed memory traces into systemic forms (such as organizational and group culture, knowledge, and skills). Webster (2011) modifies the definition of structures as "macrolevel constructs such as language, routines of work and leisure, technologies, and institutions" (p. 47). We use language and new media as resources to repackage spreadable media as memes in participatory digital culture. Giddens defines system as normalized social practices resulting from recursively reproduced actions between agents. As individuals continually interact within participatory digital culture, structuration informs us of their recursive relationship with the resources they use for meme creation. The relationship is recursive primarily because memes as genre are akin to a continued conversation between and among members of participatory digital culture. System and structure coalesce as structuration: a process by which a system is maintained through the use or application of structures.

Duality of Structure

The interaction between agent and structure represents a reciprocally constitutive duality. Structuration suggests that human agency perpetually produces, reproduces, and transforms social institutions (understood following Giddens as "structures") (Cho & Lee, 2008; Giddens,

1979; Orlikowski, 2000). Likewise, participatory digital culture recursively produces memes which "mutually reproduce the social world" (Webster, 2011, p. 45) precisely because the rules and resources available for remix, iteration, and rapid diffusion are unique to the new media landscape.

Within the duality of structure, a confluence of social and individual existence is co-constructed online as artifacts of participatory digital culture. Social structures initiate social action; concurrently, social action leads to social structures. Given the Ducreux meme, members of participatory digital culture view further iterations with enjoyment and are simultaneously cognizant of how to create another iteration; thus, the cycle continues (refer to Figures 3.1–3.3 for examples). Persistence in the generation of memes is a symptom of the reciprocally constitutive duality. It is in the recursive action that helps to reconstitute the duality of structure that memes are propagated. Memes are enacted by agents participating in normalized social practices which recursively reconstitute the structure. This in turn makes it possible for further memetic creation as long as the practices are needed. In structuration, rules are a component of structures but are not fixed (Giddens, 1979, p. 104). Accordingly, we already see memes, as we have come to know them, deployed in offline spaces such as marketing and advertising campaigns (discussed in greater detail in Chapter 5), and we may see memes proliferate in magazines, video games, children's books, films, etc. In other words, where we deploy memes is susceptible to transformation and this is invariably tied to the quality of *memes-as-genre*.

Maintenance, Elaboration, Modification: A Genre Development of Memes

Barley and Tolbert (1988, p. 9) propose "three modes of enacting already-established social institutions – maintenance, elaboration, and modification – which can be used to understand the production and reproduction of genres" (in Yates & Orlikowski, 1992, p. 306). When individuals engage in communication, an array of tools, or media, are available from which to choose to encode a message, transmit it, and possibly wait for a response. Yates and Orlikowski (1992) state that genres are social institutions which are produced, reproduced, and/or transformed when individuals communicate. From a structurational perspective, memes are messages that operate within social structures comprised of discourses.

It is my proposition that internet memes follow a genre development featuring stages of maintenance, elaboration, and modification. In structurational terms, maintenance of existing genres occurs when adherence to the rules for creating the genre is maintained without altering the genre. Furthermore, when new circumstances emerge that demand a slight adjustment of genre rules, individuals can elaborate the existing genre rules. Finally, when new circumstances emerge that demand a substantial and consistent departure from existing genre rules, individuals may choose to modify the genre. For memes, a similar development follows this pattern.

Memes are a genre, not a medium, of online communication and are artifacts of participatory digital culture characterized specifically by an agency of consumption-production. As noted by Bakhtin and Medvedev (1985), "[e]ach genre possesses definite principles of selection, definite forms for seeing and conceptualizing reality, and a definite scope and depth of penetration" (p. 131). Kamberlis (1999) furthers this point by acknowledging that texts of various kinds are produced, reproduced, distributed, and received according to their genre. As Milner (2012) notes, "memes are pop culture artifacts [and as such] they can provide insight into how 'everyday' media texts intertwine with public discourses" (p. 9).

Internet memes start in the maintenance mode as spreadable media, a term borrowed from Jenkins (2009) but modified here to mean mediated digital content which individuals can alter, if they choose, and spread again. Without spreadable media, the meme cannot exist as a genre of communication. As Carter and Arroyo (2011) explain, spreadable media imply permeation through social networks. Once individuals alter spreadable media, it develops further into an emergent meme. Finally, after remix and imitation (Milner, 2012; Shifman, 2012), and rapid diffusion (Shifman, 2013) across online spaces, the emergent meme becomes the internet meme, in the current parlance of online communication.

Spreadable Media

Multimedia messages consumed without alteration are spreadable media and are not restricted to online spaces but possess the capacity for broad distribution. As a specific example of spreadable media, consider a film trailer such as *Avengers: Infinity Wars*. In this example, I use the trailer which Marvel Studios uploaded to its YouTube page on 29 November 2017. It is important to note that movie trailers, however, do inspire participation such as the genre of dynamic reaction videos when people simply upload videos of themselves watching a trailer to reveal their own (often emotional) reaction. The term spreadable media with relation to the example of a movie trailer simply acknowledges that individuals, in this case viewers, can spread the trailer for the purpose of sharing the message further, in an effort, perhaps, to broaden the experience afforded by the viewing of the trailer. As an example of spreadable media, the *Avengers: Infinity Wars* trailer is maintained through consumption characterized by views and shares. No alteration takes place; it remains spreadable media. As of this writing, the trailer has been viewed over

200 million times. However, once spreadable media are altered, they become emergent in the elaboration mode.

Video memes develop from broadcast news (*Sweet Brown, Antoine Dodson – Bed Intruder*), user-generated videos (*Leave Britney Alone*), and uploads to sites such as YouTube (*Double Rainbow, Numa Numa, Somebody Touch My Spaghet, Ben Swolo*), and as Shifman (2014b, p. 4) notes "almost every major public event sprouts a stream of memes" thus prompting a *hypermemetic* discourse. For the purposes of analysis and addressing the matter of memes-as-genre, two examples will be discussed, namely *Distracted Boyfriend* and *The Most Interesting Man in the World*.

Emergent Meme

When spreadable media are altered, remixed, parodied, and so on, they become the emergent meme. Its characteristics include viral spread and a degree of popularity among members of participatory digital culture. However, emergent memes differ from what is commonly referred to as internet memes. Emergent memes are altered spreadable media yet are not iterated and remixed further as separate contributions. A remix or alteration becomes a separate contribution when awareness, distribution, and modification reach a critical mass (though ambiguous, this should be understood as a theoretical explanation for an ongoing phenomenon). The importance of this category is explained below.

Some spreadable media which are altered may remain stationary as emergent memes. Examples may include Bad Lip Reading (BLR), Rage Comics, and http://www.ytmnd.com (you're the man now, dog). Still some emergent memes are remixed, iterated, and distributed further thus becoming memes. Burgess and Green (2009), Knobel and Lankshear (2007), Milner (2012), and Shifman (2014a,b) have discussed memes which are largely humorous or non-critical of politics or society in general. However, the term "emergent meme" also includes subversive and/or countercultural elaborations of spreadable media. Countercultural and socially critical messages from subvertising and culture jamming are emergent memes. The rationale for their inclusion is based on the definition of emergent memes as being altered spreadable media representing the elaboration mode in the genre development of Internet memes. Culture jamming is a remix or repurposing of a known image such as a corporate logo and infuses critical perspectives on mainstream trademarks and logos. Subvertising, a portmanteau of subversion and advertising, is a related concept which seeks to evoke cognitive dissonance through the purposeful subversion of an advertisement by adding politically motivated criticism or satire but maintaining the most recognizable elements. Historically both terms are variations of *détournement*, which was a strategy espoused by the Situationist International and a concept attributed to Guy Debord (1967). Indeed, the emergent meme is the ideal vehicle for culture jamming and similar forms of *détournement* given the emphasis on condensed visualization of the object or idea that is under scrutiny.

What separates culture jamming from other emergent memes such as Rage Comics, http://www.ytmnd.com (you're the man now dog), or BLR, is the explicit socially and/or politically conscious network behind the alteration. We become duped by the culture jam emergent memes. We see the hijacked Tommy Hilfiger or Obsession for Women ads from Adbusters.org, and realize that its form exists as an advertisement yet we are simultaneously made aware of a remixing of the ad into a subversive or countercultural, socially critical message. The culture jammed emergent meme differs from BLR in that BLR is a stationary parody defined by a one-time alteration of a specific movie trailer, political speech, and so on and no further alterations or remixes of BLR videos take place. Ron English's attempts to professionalize culture jamming through his work in "popaganda" are similar to BLR in the one-time alteration of well-known products or corporate logos. His mash-ups of high and low culture equally dupe its audience as in the examples from Adbusters.

Arguably other, perhaps more popular emergent memes that do not use culture jamming as a central message are distinguished by levity and humor in most if not all instances. It is unwise to characterize all emergent memes as being humorous, but an element in remixing spreadable media seems to be a desire for levity.

Central to the emergent meme is alteration which is warranted due to a quality in spreadable media and the technologies used to access them which invites individuals to alter spreadable media into emergent memes. Emergent memes exist as a direct consequence of agency within the digital culture. This progression from spreadable media to memes is a symptom of the dynamic interaction between agency and structure, central to structuration theory.

Internet Meme

The emergent becomes the internet meme after participatory digital culture has produced imitations, remixes, and further iterations of the emergent meme. Memes are rapidly diffused online especially via online social networks. The imitated meme is iterated to create new memes continuing the cycle of genre development. The distance between elaboration and modification is scant but is nearly impenetrable without transgression through intentional imitation, iteration, and rapid diffusion. The genre development as proposed may appear rather rigid upon consideration of the preponderance of memes in contemporary digital society. It is, however, my contention that viewing memes developmentally assists in situating their purpose within discourse. The following sections introduce the memes analyzed according to the genre development.

Distracted Boyfriend

With respect to the genre development of memes, the *Distracted Boyfriend* meme started as spreadable media in the form of a stock image originally taken by photographer Antonio Guillem uploaded to *iStock* in 2015 (Knowyourmeme.com, 2017). Further stock photos in the series reveal the troubled couple splitting up only to have the two young women befriending each other and engaging in romance. Figure 3.4 shows a remix of the meme posted to Nigel Farage's Facebook page on the question of Brexit and the potential interest for Italy to cede from the union as well. The title of the source image was "disloyal man with his girlfriend looking at another girl", which internet users truncated to *Distracted Boyfriend* for myriad uses starting at least as early as 2017 on a Turkish Facebook page by the name of Prog Düşmanlarına Verilen Müthiş Cevaplar.

With the *Distracted Boyfriend* meme, the insertion of text may have originated on the Turkish Facebook page and posted on January 30, 2017. Its utility was to critique pop music from the standpoint of progressive musicians, such as Phil Collins, depicted in the remixed stock photo as the distracted boyfriend. The meme typically shows a young man, walking and holding hands with a young woman who is presumed to be his girlfriend, turning around to check out the body of another woman walking away from the couple and toward the viewer.

The *Distracted Boyfriend* image has developed into multipurpose sub-genre of memes known as *object labeling*. Typically, the semiotic

Figure 3.4 Distracted Boyfriend Posted to Nigel Farage's Facebook Page.

function of the image utilizes the gaze of the individuals in the image to tell a brief story, often with or without text. Another example is actually included in Chapter 4 and shown in Figure 4.2. That version uses no text but deploys the flag of Catalonia and Spain and the face of embattled politician Carles Puigdemont in order to criticize his decision to leave Spain for Belgium during the Catalonian independence movement in 2017. Regardless of the particular instance, one reason why the image of the young man looking with interest at another woman is perhaps also due to the cultural assumption that men are more likely to be disloyal than women. Interestingly, the photographer who took the image that became the *Distracted Boyfriend* meme had already uploaded a similar photograph with the gender roles reversed. In this instance, a young man's girlfriend is looking astray at another young man in the foreground. It may be pure chance that what became the *Distracted Boyfriend* meme originated as the image it is, but I suspect that the cultural assumption mentioned above likely had greater communicative salience and thus more utility in creating *new* narratives by remixing the meme iteratively.

The Most Interesting Man in the World

"He is the most interesting man in the world" or so he was introduced as part of a successful and innovative advertising campaign in 2006 by Euro RSCG Worldwide, a global marketing firm (Knowyourmeme. com, 2013b). American actor Jonathan Goldsmith portrayed "the most interesting man" who popularized the self-aggrandizing commercials during which Goldsmith's character makes a statement that was later remixed by participatory digital culture ("I don't always drink beer, but when I do, I prefer Dos Equis – Stay thirsty, my friends"). At some point between 2007 and 2009, the first image macro memes appeared featuring Goldsmith's character (see Figure 3.5 for an example). The catchphrase omitted the appeal to purchase Dos Equis beer but kept the self-referentiality. The transgression from broadcast television to image macro meme suggests that the TV commercial campaign as spreadable media evoked a response from participatory digital culture. This is an example of development from spreadable media to emergent meme with nearly immediate development into meme. It is difficult to ascertain exactly when the spreadable media became emergent. It is, however, likely that it was easier for participatory digital culture to remix the TV commercial as an image macro. With an image macro meme, individuals are able to quickly re-visit the ongoing conversation and contribute to it with more, related image macro memes. Users remixing the meme largely adhere to the prescriptive phrasal template '*I don't always do X, but when I do, I do Y*'.

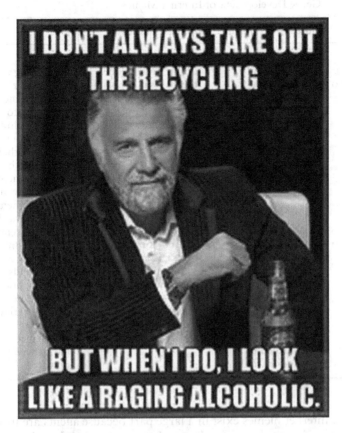

Figure 3.5 The Most Interesting Man in the World.

Structuration in the Context of Internet Memes

It is advisable to demonstrate the progression from spreadable media, emergent meme, and finally to meme by providing case studies on two specific memes, namely, *The Most Interesting Man in the World* and *Distracted Boyfriend*. The first choice started as a video and then maintained stability as a sub-genre in the form of an image macro, whereas the second is an image macro meme which tends to use the direction of the gaze as an integral component in understanding the semiotic items inserted for meaning making. The progression is succinctly presented in Table 3.1.

Recalling Giddens, systems emerge as normalized social practices enacted through recursively reproduced agential actions. Agents recursively reproduce their actions in the consumption and production of memes as if involved in a conversation between members of participatory digital

Table 3.1 Genre Development of Internet Memes

	Spreadable Media	Emergent Meme	Meme
Video/ image macro	Television commercial advertising Dos Equis beer features Jonathan Goldsmith as *The Most Interesting Man in the World* (2006)	Image macros appear online and include the phrasal template *I don't always X, but when I do, I Y* (2007–2009)	*The Most Interesting Man in the World* meme continues to have the phrasal template but includes other images such as the Ancient Aliens Guy and Ducreux memes (2010 onward)
Image macro	Photographer Antonion Guillem's stock photo entitled "disloyal man with his girlfriend looking at another girl" uploaded to iStock in 2015	Possibly the Turkish Facebook page Prog Düşmanlarına Verilen Müthiş Cevaplar and their remix of the image to critique Phil Collins in January 2017	Subsequent remixes of the *Distracted Boyfriend* meme which tends to incorporate text and/or image-overlays to extend the memetic narrative 2017 onward

culture. Internet memes exist in a large part because agents are involved in the recursive production and reproduction of memes but also because the structures enacted by the agential creation of memes lead to the further reproduction of memes. Memes continue to be created as long as agential practical consciousness is defined by a desire for memetic content to be remixed, iterated, and distributed further. It is not a system bound by immutable rules, however. Memetic systems are defined by the presence of an emergent meme (an altered form of spreadable media) that is recursively reproduced in a process in which agents adhere to an unstated but known structure. Giddens uses the term *memory traces* to describe structure (Giddens, 1984). In memetic terms, memory traces (or structures) are the procedures of designing specific memetic content in such a way to be recognized as memes in order to promote a recursive reconstitution of related memes. In the case of *The Most Interesting Man in the World*, memory traces let individuals know what to do in order to participate; that is, to recognize a particular message as a meme and, if desired, to reproduce similar memetic content in the hopes of a repeated process of recognition and reproduction. Both *The Most Interesting Man in the World* and *Distracted Boyfriend* contain the rules and resources necessary for further remix. Memory traces (or structures) may be active or dormant and therefore are drawn upon when individuals wish to further the conversation. In the case of *The Most Interesting Man in the World*, the generative power of the phrasal template is limited only by the creativity of participatory digital culture. For *Distracted Boyfriend*, iterations tend to use the *direction* of the gaze of the three individuals in the image and also inserted text, images, or other media for discursive purposes.

Memes require the abstraction inherent in Giddens' structuration theory in order for researchers to make sense of the apparent randomness by which they are produced and reproduced by participatory digital culture. Giddens notes that "[s]ociety only has form, and that form only has effects on people, insofar as structure is produced and reproduced in what people do" (Giddens & Pierson, 1998, p. 77). Similarly, agents draw upon structures (memory traces) when they are needed.

Memetic transformation is the origin of structuration's relevance to memes. As in the case of the popular Ducreux meme mentioned at the beginning of the chapter, agential action recursively produces memes and reproduces the means by which it should be reconstituted.

Structuration offers an internal view of memetic creation. The presence of a meme implies that agents actively draw on structures recursively and that structures regulate such action, hence the duality of structure (and agency). Agential action on the memescape implies not only the creation of memes but of structures associated with memes which then recursively constitute the structure in which the agential action takes place. Once spreadable media become emergent, and further, once the emergent gains the attention needed in order to become remixed and iterated, a meme is realized.

Concluding Discussion

Memes as artifacts of participatory digital culture illustrate the duality of structure in that they possess the instructions on how to remix and reproduce themselves while they simultaneously evince the agential activity needed for their reproduction. The literature on internet memes lacks a theoretical framework. This contribution establishes a few steps forward in that direction. The proposed genre development of internet memes introduces three categories to describe memetic transformation: spreadable media, emergent meme, and meme. This analysis argues that memes are remixed and iterated messages which are rapidly spread by members of participatory digital culture. Memes develop from emergent memes, defined as altered or remixed spreadable media.

This analysis benefits from the inclusion of Giddens' structuration theory as it is useful in addressing how memes are created and how the process of genre development demonstrates the generative capacity both for continued memetic transformation and participation from members of digital culture. Structuration positions these dynamic components as the core of a duality of structure and agency for internet memes. Furthermore, Gidden's structuration theory can serve as a model to further analyze the spread and development of memes, answering such questions as how online communities develop and legitimize genre conventions for memes, how memes are used in different cultures with differing social and political contexts, and to identify the main forces shaping the genre of new and emergent memes.

Do All Memes Follow the Genre Development?

In closing, I must acknowledge the limitations of the approach to understanding how internet memes develop. On the one hand, when something occurs in the real world that results in the creation of internet memes as a kind of discursive response, we can follow the development of memes in terms of people purposefully selecting spreadable media, augmenting it, sharing it online for mass consumption. On the other hand, sometimes memes are just memes – in the common digital parlance *meme* is understood rather broadly, and this understanding has implications worthy of consideration. For example, the Facebook page *Classical Art Memes*, is followed by over 5 million others on Facebook. The point of *Classical Art Memes* is largely humorous, and this factor may explain the high number of followers as well as active engagement (in terms of likes, shares, etc. of a given post). As an applied example, I will discuss two image-macro memes posted to the Facebook page on March 20, 2018. The first is a remixed rendering of German painter Carl Spitzberg's *Der Bücherwurm*, or the bookworm, from approximately 1850, and the second is a remixed version of Vincent Van Gogh's *Starry Night* from 1889.

The primary approach to meme creation on *Classical Art Memes* is the insertion of text for humorous effect. The Spitzweg painting-as-meme acknowledges the contemporary deployment of memes as a form of utterance, a visual counterpart to verbal language in online spaces. The Spitzweg painting-as-meme garnered over 88,000 Facebook reactions and 20,000 shares, whereas the Van Gogh painting-as-meme gained over 96,000 reactions and 25,000 shares in less than two days since they were posted. The point here is that while my deliberation on memes as genre is helpful to the understanding of how memes develop in general and with specific reference to the importance of being able to track such development, memes may emerge in altogether different ways, as depicted on *Classical Art Memes*.

I have argued that memes, when viewed as a genre, develop from spreadable media, to emergent memes, and finally to internet memes. With examples such as *Classical Art Memes* obviously, I must adjust my position, at least somewhat. In a strict sense, the genre development

I have proposed reveals the process by which non-viral, commonplace, spreadable media can become memes, and this process reveals how individuals within participatory digital culture use media discursively. However, we can also view the memes shared on *Classical Art Memes* in a similar light. The Van Gogh painting-as-meme, for example, poses a humorous remixing of one of the most recognizable works of art but also inheres a politically critical aspect, namely, the implied criticism of the military of the USA and its deployment in the Middle East. The implied interpretation of the meme is that the US military will seek out and combat entities who possess oil. But what of the process of genre development? By implication, all or most of the memes posted to the *Classical Art Memes* page are digital versions of artworks – thus they are all already spreadable media. The addition of text is a remixing; we can see this as a quick entry into the elaboration mode, or as I have rephrased it here, the turning from spreadable media into an emergent meme. Perhaps, it is sufficient to simply acknowledge, as was alluded to earlier, that it is advisable to view the distance between the emergent meme and internet meme as a kind of thin membrane, and the evolution from emergent to internet meme can occur with such rapidity, its usefulness in such examples is redundant.

However, the paintings-as-meme in these examples clearly are internet memes precisely because of the interaction and engagement they provoke and encourage as well as the use of the meme itself in ensuing discursive activity, such as in comments posted to the meme. In many instances, such as with the more political Van Gogh painting-as-meme, arguments ensue with respect to a need for military action, increase or decrease in spending, gun control, etc., but concurrent with the general sentiments expressed therein remains an acknowledgement of the source of the discussion, namely the meme itself.

Of course, we can also say that the Van Gogh painting-as-meme is itself simply a reaction to an already existing situation, that is, the perception of US military as positive or negative in incursions in the Middle East, etc., but it is sufficient here to view it as a source of the discussion given the structure in inhabits, namely a Facebook page dedicated to posting (mostly humorous) image-macro memes remixed from classical art. In closing, and to elucidate on a point that may not be entirely clear, if I were to post an image-macro painting-as-meme to the *Classical Art Memes* page and it garnered zero reactions, shares, and comments, is it still a meme? According to my own definition of internet memes, my articulation of memes as artifacts of digital culture, and how others have defined memes, the answer is clearly "no". To answer in the affirmative would be to ignore agency – the agential interaction to further the message, react to it, remix it and share it, etc. For memes to be memes, people must have some role in responding to them. This is also a clear indication of the separation between the Dawkinsian meme, which emphasizes imitation and replication – not necessarily remix and parody – and the internet meme, which functions enthymemetically as a visual argument necessitating an audience – imagined or otherwise – to fill in missing or absent messages in order for the meme to exist. The following chapter presents a series of case studies as part of a larger exploration of political internet memes.

Note

1   Note: Much of the content of this chapter was originally published in the journal *New Media & Society* and appears here with permission from the editor. The original work was written by two individuals and is referenced as: Wiggins, B. E., & Bowers, G. B. (2014). Memes as genre: A structurational analysis of the memescape. *New Media & Society, 17*, 1886–1906. doi:10.1177/1461444814535194.

References

Archer, M. (1995). *Realist social theory: The morphogenetic approach.* Cambridge: Cambridge University Press.

Bakhtin, M. M., & Medvedev, P. N. (1985). *The formal method in literary scholarship: A critical introduction to sociological poetics* (A. J. Werhle, Trans.). Cambridge, MA: Harvard University Press.

Barley, S. R., & Tolbert, P. S. (1988). Institutionalization as structuration: Methods and analytic strategies for studying links between action and structure. *Conference on longitudinal field research methods for studying organizational processes.* Austin: University of Texas.

Bazerman, C., & Russell, D. (2003). *Writing selves/writing societies: Research from activity perspectives on writing.* Fort Collins, CO: The WAC Clearinghouse and Mind, Culture, and Activity. Retrieved from http://wac.colostate.edu/books/selves_societies/

Burgess, J., & Green, J. (2009). *YouTube: Online video and participatory culture.* Malden, MA: Polity.

Carter, G. V., & Arroyo, S. J. (2011). Tubing the future: Participatory pedagogy and YouTube U in 2020. *Computers and Composition, 28*, 292–302.

Cho, H., & Lee, J. (2008). Collaborative information seeking in intercultural computer-mediated communication groups. *Communication Research, 35*(4), 548–573.

Debord, G. (1967). *The society of the spectacle.* Retrieved from http://www.marxists.org/reference/archive/debord/society.htm

DeSanctis, G., & Poole, M. (1994). Capturing the complexity in advanced technology use: Adaptive structuration theory. *Organization Science, 5*(2), 121–147.

Eco, U. (1984). *Semiotics and the philosophy of language.* Hong Kong: Macmillan.

Falkheimer, J. (2009). On Giddens: Interpreting public relations through Anthony Giddens' structuration and late modernity theory. In O. Ihlen, B. van

Ruler, & M. Frederiksson (Eds.), *Public relations and social theory: Key figures and concepts* (pp. 103–119). New York: Routledge.

Giddens, A. (1979). *Central problems in social theory*. Berkeley and Los Angeles: University of California Press.

Giddens, A. (1984). *The constitution of society: Outline of the theory of structure*. Berkeley: University of California Press.

Giddens, A., & Pierson, C. (1998). *Conversations with Anthony Giddens: Making sense of modernity*. Stanford, CA: Stanford University Press.

Goffman, E. (1956). *The presentation of self in everyday life*. Garden City, NY: Doubleday.

Jenkins, H. (2009, February 11). *If it doesn't spread, it's dead (part one): Media viruses and memes. Confessions of an Aca-Fan* [Web log]. Retrieved from http://henryjenkins.org/2009/02/if_it_doesnt_spread_its_dead_p.html

Kamberlis, G. (1995). Genre as institutionally informed social practice. *Journal of Contemporary Legal Issues, 6*(115), 115–171.

Kamberlis, G. (1999). Genre development and learning: Children writing stories, science reports, and poems. *Research in the Teaching of English, 33,* 403–460.

Knobel, M., & Lankshear, C. (2007). *A new literacies sampler*. New York: Peter Lang.

Knowyourmeme.com (2013a). *Ducreux.* Retrieved from http://knowyourmeme.com/memes/joseph-ducreux-archaic-rap

Knowyourmeme.com (2013b). *The most interesting man in the world.* Retrieved from http://knowyourmeme.com/memes/the-most-interesting-man-in-the-world

Knowyourmeme.com (2017). *Distracted boyfriend.* Retrieved from http://knowyourmeme.com/memes/distracted-boyfriend

Miller, C.R. (1984). Genre as social action. *Quarterly Journal of Speech, 7*(1984), 151–167.

Milner, R. M. (2012). *The world made meme: Discourse and identity in participatory media* (PhD thesis). The University of Kansas, Lawrence, KS.

Orlikowski, W. J. (1992). The duality of technology: Rethinking the concept of technology in organizations. *Organization Science, 3*(3), 398–427.

Orlikowski, W. J. (2000). Using technology and constituting structures: A practice lens for studying technology in organizations. *Organization Science, 11*(4), 404–428.

Parsons, T. (1951). *The social system.* New York: The Free Press.

Pavlou, P. A., & Majchrzak, A. (2002). Structuration theory: Capturing the complexity of business-to-business intermediaries. In M. Warkentin (Ed.), *Business to business electronic commerce: Challenges & solutions* (pp. 175–189). Hershey, PA: Idea Group Publishing.

Poole, M. S., Seibold, D. R., & McPhee, R. D. (1996). The structuration of group decisions. In R. Y. Hirokawa & M. S. Poole (Eds.), *Communication and group decision making* (pp. 114–146). Thousand Oaks, CA: Sage.

Shifman, L. (2012). Anatomy of a YouTube meme. *New Media & Society, 14*(2), 187–203.

Shifman, L. (2013). Memes in a digital world: Reconciling with a conceptual troublemaker. *Journal of Computer-Mediated Communication, 18,* 362–377.

Shifman, L. (2014a). The cultural logic of photo-based meme genres. *Journal of Visual Culture, 13*(3), 340–357.

Shifman, L. (2014b). *Memes in digital culture.* Cambridge: MIT Press.

Stones, R. (2005). *Structuration theory.* New York: Palgrave Macmillan.

Todorov, T. (1990). *Genres in discourse.* Cambridge: Cambridge University Press.

Tucker, K. H. (1998). *Anthony Giddens and modern social theory.* Thousand Oaks, CA: Sage.

Waldeck, J. H., Shepard, C. A., Teitelbaum, J., Farrar, W. J., & Seibold, D. R. (2002). New directions for functional, symbolic convergence, structuration, and bona fide group perspectives of group communication. In L. R. Frey (Ed.), *New directions in group communication* (pp. 3–25). Thousand Oaks, CA: Sage.

Wartofsky, M. W. (1979). *Models: Representation and scientific understanding.* Dordrecht: Reidel.

Watts, R. J. (1981). *The pragmalinguistic analysis of narrative texts.* Tübingen: Gunter Narr Verlag.

Webster, J. G. (2011). The duality of media: A structurational theory of public attention. *Communication Theory, 21,* 43–66.

Wiggins, B. E., & Bowers, G. B. (2014). Memes as genre: A structurational analysis of the memescape. *New Media & Society, 17,* 1886–1906. doi:10.1177/1461444814535194

Yates, J., & Orlikowski, W. J. (1992). Genres of organizational communication: A structurational approach to studying communication and media. *Academy of Management Review, 17*(2), 299–326.

4 Political Memes

Dedicating a chapter to the meaningful ways in which internet memes are deployed for and/or about political purposes reflects recent changes in the political landscape in the USA and globally. However, it also highlights the pervasiveness of memes as a tool for quick and succinct online expression. What distinguishes this contribution from previous works on memes and politics is the deliberation with regard to ideological practice as semiotically constructed and often involving intertextual references to popular culture.

Specifically, this chapter focuses on a handful of case studies in which the deployment of internet memes in political campaigns or related purposes reveals a deeper look into the discursive power of memes in digital culture. The movement for Catalonian independence in Spain is at the center of the first case study. This is followed by the second case study which examines how internet memes were used by a Russian-based internet agency during the lead up to the 2016 US presidential election. This analysis also reveals intriguing parallels between what historian Timothy Snyder calls the *politics of eternity* and the semiotic construction of Russian internet memes on social media ahead of the 2018 Russian presidential election. The third and final case study handles the use of memes in China, but its emphasis is less on actual memes (though a few are mentioned) and more on what the implications of censoring internet memes signifies for digital culture(s). The work of French philosopher Jean Baudrillard is incorporated in the analyses as his concepts (*simulacra* and the *hyperreal*) offer insightful opportunities to understand the function of internet memes deployed for political purposes – at least restricted to the examples included in the case studies. A general review of research on *international* uses of internet memes offers a good foundation prior to the case study sections. An initial analysis of the so-called *Obama Joker* meme from 2009, and the ostensibly positive remixing of the Batman villain for Trump in 2016, precedes the case studies.

Technological Affordances and Ideological Practice

The choice among members of participatory digital culture to express their agreement or rejection of political realities in the form of internet memes reflects the technological affordances of the internet in a world beset by political change. With the rise of mobile telephony and the preponderance of apps that allow users to take photos, augment both image and video, quickly edit and upload, stream live videos, etc. the average person is technologically enabled to add to a chorus of digital content – regardless of the merit of a particular contribution. This trend is not necessarily new, especially with regard to the intersection of political forms of communication and speculative or even conspiratorial lines of thought. For example, personal photographic and video cameras fueled conjecture about the Zapruder film which captured the assassination of John F. Kennedy. What is striking about the Zapruder example is how reality can be recorded yet the result is necessarily up to the interpretation ascribed to it as a construction of reality (and not reality itself). Similarly, the film series *Loose Change* (2005–2009) offered conspiratorial approaches to define the events around September 11, 2001 despite various authorities having since debunked the claims made in the films. Personal computers and video editing software enable individuals to augment found footage in order to produce wildly speculative claims that adhere to a paranoid and/or conspiratorial line of thought. A tendency to create or promote conspiracy theories exists when individuals attempt to make sense of an event or the larger world when, for them, meaning is simply out of reach.

The technological affordances of the internet, while at once seemingly awe-inspiring, also enable anyone with a particular view, especially a marginalized, less mainstream perspective to produce content that conforms to their own ideological practice, thus encouraging others with consonant views to consume and spread the same content. In the USA, for example, the emergence of the *Black Lives Matter* movement was met with a counter-movement called *Blue Lives Matter*, which ostensibly supports the police side of the issue and de-emphasizes claims of racism as articulated by *Black Lives Matter*. Indeed, in a study conducted by Bock and Figueroa (2017, p. 1), "the two groups' [*Black Lives Matter* and *Blue Lives* Matter] symbol systems are homologous with larger, ideological tensions in American culture: faith and reason". However, while these preliminary examples obviously point to serious issues of ideological practice with real-world implications, some internet memes that address political issues embrace levity perhaps for the purpose of defusing a tense situation, as in the case of the Catalonian call for independence from Spain, to be discussed in a later section. It is important to first briefly review previous scholarship on internet memes and politics.

International Research into Internet Memes

A tendency exists in internet meme scholarship to focus on memes from the standpoint of the USA, however voices from countries other than the USA are also producing contributions on internet memes and culture, politics, and more. For example, Ekdale and Tully (2013) examine the ways in which internet users in Kenya appropriated Kenyan popular culture to "reappropriate stereotypes of weakness into aspirations of strength" (p. 1). Their discussion of the *Makmende* meme reveals how participatory digital culture transgresses geographic and temporal boundaries. Kligler-Vilenchik and Thorson (2015) discuss the Kony2012 meme and social change. El Khachab (2016, p. 21) examines how users in Egypt employed internet memes in order to "condense various visual techniques and joking conventions to deliver a political point concerning Egypt's electricity infrastructure".

Saito (2017) analyzes how Japanese anime is received in China and what this process reveals about matters of transnational cultural influence. Other research has examined how internet users deploy internet memes as creative expressions in order to counter censorship in China (Du, 2014; Wallis, 2011). To discuss the issue of male *homosociality* in China and how internet memes assist in the discursive practice of identity negotiation, Wei (2017) conducted interviews with undergraduate and graduate students to explore the so-called *gao-ji* discourse of gay Chinese youth.

While a common assumption may be that internet users deploy memes for humorous purposes, as has been noted thus far internet memes often include some degree of social, cultural, or political critique. Another assumption may be that, if users were to deploy memes for critical purposes, these would likely be directed at a government, organization, or similar entity. However, Pearce and Hajizada (2014) explored the use of memes *by* the government of Azerbaijan to countermand opposition.

Researchers Arestova, Balandina, and Budko (2015) investigate the origins of the internet meme in Russian culture, whereas Denisova (2014) suggests that memes are a coded language of dissent on the Russian internet. The annexation of Crimea in 2014 and the reactions of the USA, the European Union, and other countries were the source for internet memes on Twitter (Wiggins, 2014, 2016). The analysis revealed a preponderance of memes that fell into one of two categories: directionally Russian or directionally Ukrainian. Directionality as a thematic category is a novel methodological approach in memes research. While the memes reference a given news story or event, they continued to be consumed and reproduced along similar thematic categories.

In general, scholarship linking internet memes and politics tends to focus on marginalized groups. Additionally, research shows that internet memes provide a mode for talking about a political reality which may be viewed as unfavorable by the dominant governing order. Other research has shown that governments as well as political campaigns deploy internet memes for the purpose of attacking opposition as well as supporting a particular candidate. Research on memes in China (Du, 2014; Wallis, 2011) has revealed a tendency among Chinese netizens to use subversive and enigmatic phrasing in order to avoid censorship. Wallis found that netizens used words or images of a *river crab* online since the phrase is homophonous with the Chinese word for *harmony*, however both concepts use different characters. Wallis (2011) found that "[b]ecause the word for harmony or harmonious is so frequently used sarcastically online, it is often censored, and thus those who are discussing censorship use the characters for river crab" in order to express some form of dissent (p. 425).

Following the announcement of Xi Jinping's potential indefinite rule as the Chinese leader, censorship authorities in China have aggressively removed images and phrases used to mock or criticize Xi, the decision of National People's Congress to cease term limits, or Chinese politics in general. Several dual-panel image memes portray Xi as the cartoon character Winnie the Pooh, ostensibly a reference to the leader's physical attributes. In addition to blocking the Pooh meme, the following phrases were also censored on Weibo, China's version of Twitter, and elsewhere in online Chinese spaces: "I don't agree"; "migration"; "emigration"; "re-election"; "election term"; "constitution amendment"; "constitution rules"; and "proclaiming oneself an emperor" (Allen, 2018; Brimelow, 2018). A later section will examine the implications of meaning contained in the censored internet memes.

On the flipside, governments have also deployed memes against opposition. The government of Azerbaijan used memes to countermand opposition according to research conducted by Pearce and Hajizada (2014). The authors also found that the history of using humor as a form of dissent in Azerbaijan is a rich and storied one. To understand the governmental motivations in deploying memes to attack opposition, Pearce and Hajizada incorporate Edward Schatz's *soft authoritarian toolkit* to analyze the government's approaches. The authors (2014) found that

> [i]nternet memes are exemplary for this task because they provide an opportunity to show support (through 'likes' and 'shares'); they often are part of larger blackmail campaigns; they are harassing; they help the regime control the narrative; and they stage political drama. (p. 78)

Before proceeding to the case studies, it is advisable to review the ways in which attitudes toward memes and their involvement in political discourse has changed in academic literature. This is an important point as the tendency not to take memes seriously as tools for political expression was general practice in years past.

Jokerizing Obama: Appropriations of Meaning

Whitney Phillips (2009) deliberated on the question of the so-called *Obama Joker* meme that emerged in early 2009. She sought to understand the meaning of the merging of the two entities, one the 44th President of the USA, the other a real person (Heath Ledger) in a fictional role as the iconic enemy of Batman, the Joker. It was unclear for most of 2009 as to who created the mash-up. Finally, in mid-August, just days after Phillips' own musings on the subject were posted to Henry Jenkins' blog, it was revealed that a then-20-year-old Palestinian-American college student named Firas Alkhateeb wanted to *jokerize* an image of Obama to offer criticism of the president (Hechtkopf, 2009; Milian, 2009). The original image was taken from a cover of Time Magazine published October 23, 2006 and then jokerized using digital editing software; it is shown in Figure 4.1.

Alkhteeb's motivations to remix the image as a reference to the Joker was simply to suggest that Obama was not a messianic figure whose message of *Hope* he viewed as strategic marketing at best. Phillips' (2009) own interpretation of the *Obama Joker* meme and its subsequent inclusion of the term *socialism* under the image suggests ideological alignment with individuals in opposition to Obama and his presidency. Further, Phillips posits that the so-called *Birther* movement, which incidentally came from Donald Trump's provocative claims from 2011 onward, substantially benefited from the deployment of the image as a rejection of Obama as president. Jenkins, Ford, and Green (2013, p. 28) build on Phillips' interpretation by stating that the use of the *Obama Joker* meme functioned as a visual form of protest especially among Tea Party groups who asserted opposition to Obama's national healthcare plan. Phillips suggests further that the *Birther* movement as well as individuals with racist tendencies deployed and/or identified with the *Obama Joker* image, especially with the added text *socialism*, as an assumption about a hidden political agenda to undermine American sovereignty. Phillips (2009, para. 13) notes that

> despite the fact that both camps have harnessed the Obama/Joker image for their own purposes, and despite the fact that no one, no one, has provided an airtight (not to mention fully coherent) account of what the Obama/Joker image is trying to express, each group has used the image to prove something nefarious about their political opponents.

What Phillips refers to here is a perceived intransigence about memes and meaning. There is an assumption that a given meme, with a specific semiotic construction, must mean something and be used in specific ways because of the needs and affordances of a particular group or community.

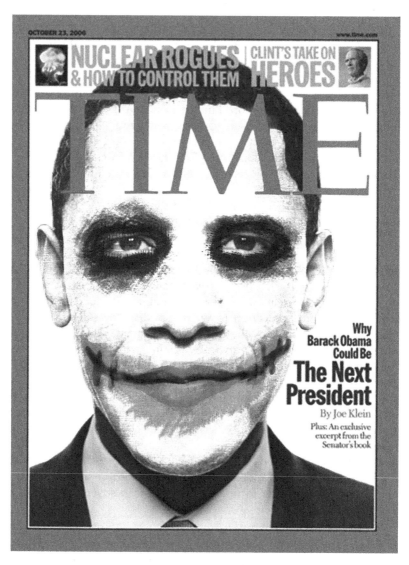

Figure 4.1 Obama, Jokerized.

Shifman (2014) notes that memes connect personal and political realities and characterizes what she refers to as "networked individualism" (p. 129). By this she means that "people use memes to simultaneously express both their uniqueness and their connectivity" (p. 30). However, what these perspectives, helpful though they are, seem to miss is that the ideological practice afforded by internet memes gains meaning only through acceptance by and incorporation into a group or community.

It is the group where interpretive salience is located. Be it the Birthers or just generally racist people for whom the *Obama Joker* meme is critical, it is their interpretation that is critical not the meme itself. What I mean by *interpretive salience* is simply that while a given meme undergoes semiotic construction consonant with a particular ideological practice, it is fallacious to think of the meme as inhering some kind of influencing power unto itself. The interpretation has salience to the group for whom a particular meme reflects a perceived ideological practice.

Ironically, the same application of the Joker to Obama was made to candidate-then-president Donald Trump in 2016. As I have noted elsewhere,

> [c]onsidering the outcome of the US presidential election and how mainstream media and major national polls collectively failed to anticipate a likely Trump win, it is especially interesting to note the saliency of Trump's depiction in the memes as a joker, wild card, and possibly as an agent of chaos.
>
> (Wiggins, 2017, p. 200)

The use of the Joker does not necessarily imply negative criticism. As noted, Phillips (2009) said that no person has been able to interpret what the *Obama Joker* meme expresses, yet simultaneously acknowledges its salience among groups whose political alignment is in gross opposition to Obama, whether due to unsupported claims as to his heritage or due to flagrant racism (given the white face in jokerizing Obama). The meaning of the *Obama Joker* meme is evident in its deployment: it is an emblem of an assumed group identity which seeks to demonstrate enmity as a part of their ideological practice. Furthermore, using the Joker to critique Obama accomplishes another association. According to Philip Kennicott (2009),

> Obama, like the Joker and like the racial stereotype of the black man, carries within him an unknowable, volatile and dangerous marker of urban violence, which could erupt at any time. The charge of socialism is secondary to the basic message that Obama can't be trusted, not because he is a politician, but because he's black.
>
> (para. 13)

Obama as Joker, Trump as Joker?

While the *Obama Joker* meme (with the added text *socialism*) demonstrates fear and anxiety about a black president, the *Trump Joker* meme champions a sublime irony. By positing Trump as an agent of chaos, his supporters feel justified by his election after 8 years of Obama. By depicting Trump as the Joker, the function is emblematic of a group which views him as a willful threat specifically positioned to undermine the status quo and inject instability in the political system.

The following sections of this chapter reveal how internet memes are deployed to criticize a politician or political movement. Further internet memes can be used at once to undermine a politician and indirectly support another. When we view the musings surrounding the *Obama Joker* meme from 2009 especially from the current political environment, assumptions that protest memes – such as the ones used in the *Birther* and *Tea Party* movements – are innocuously used ignore a principal feature of memes as artifacts of participatory culture. As noted in Chapter 3, *memory traces* support the individuals in the enactment or performance of acts based on expected social interactions within a social system and may be active or dormant (Giddens, 1984). The *Obama Joker* meme signifies the degree of impact memes can have on digital culture. Drawing on *memory traces,* individuals can use memes to re-activate ideological practice in order to reinforce a group's political understanding of itself and what it opposes. This was the case when the *Obama Joker* meme first emerged in 2009. Academics saw the use of the meme in negative terms and struggled to make sense of it. However, that meme is from a time when social media usage was not as widespread and pervasive. For example, in the fourth quarter of 2009, Facebook had approximately 360 million users, and in the fourth quarter of 2016, the number of users increased by approximately 1.5 billion (Statista, 2018). The *Obama Joker* meme was used to express an attitude about Obama which perhaps other media did not permit or which would have been more cumbersome than the simple sharing of a remixed image of the 44th President of the USA as the Batman villain, the Joker.

The *Trump Joker* meme demonstrates that memes, like language, are neutral: the meaning *ascribed* to memes is achieved *actively* by individuals and groups. This is the essence of their discursive power. The directionality of a particular meme is important insofar as to understand that a given meme, especially political ones, will likely appeal to an already-existing attitude, assumption, prejudice, fear, point of pride, conspiracy theory, value, etc. to achieve salience within a given group. *Memory traces* enable internet memes to be used and understood as emblematic of a particular group's political orientation to or opposition of a person, event, movement, etc.

What Exactly is a *Political* Meme?

First, it is important to define *politics*, and Blattberg's (2001) parsimonious phrasing is sufficient for this purpose: "politics consists of responding to conflict with dialogue" (p. 193). Individuals may choose to deploy political memes not to respond to conflict but rather to engage in and to extend conflict through discursive practice.

Viewed as a practical, enacted process, politics is akin to a continuous debate or argument "about what we should do as a nation and how it should be done, where the rules by which we argue may themselves become part of the argument" (Boynton, 2004, p. 299). Accordingly, memes deployed with regard to the political process should fundamentally inhere some form of argument. As noted in Chapter 1, we should move away from the Dawkinsian variant of memes as *mimema*, or the replicated or imitated thing, and embrace *enthymeme* as the etymological derivative of what we commonly understand to be internet memes. As such, memes as enthymemes are visual arguments that suggest a message whose comprehension and reception are dependent upon the viewer's ability to fill in necessary but absent information.

A political meme is a sub-genre of the internet meme and addresses some aspect of political philosophy and ideology. Here, the terms political philosophy and ideology require some clarification.

Blattberg (2001, p. 194) defines a political philosophy as a system of thought that offers "accounts of certain modes of political justification", such as governance, recognition, and welfare, but does so in rather general ways. A political ideology is more pragmatic and normative, here the term ideology is applied in the tradition as it was originally introduced by French philosopher Destutt de Tracy as a science of ideas. "[W]hen values or goals conflict, those who respond by invoking ideology assert at least two" perspectives (Blattberg, 2001, p. 194). The first is concerned with how those values and goals should be understood (e.g. liberty, marriage, etc.). The second asserts what the proper relationship between values and goals should be. Whether it is an image macro meme of a politician alongside a (widely recognizable) character from popular culture or a remixing of a standard political, image-based message in order to lampoon and undermine the political referent organization, we are speaking of political internet memes. However, there must be some argument or purpose (contained within the meme) for it to be political. Further, the argument must be constructed with regard to a particular political view, how to respond to a political actor or other entity, the proposal or rejection of or support for legislation, the advocacy for and exercise of force and security, the promotion of peace or war, or simply to accuse political agents of maleficence, corruption, incompetence, etc.

The gravity of political memes is dependent upon the degree of perceived importance about the given issue. For example, a meme that remixed the assassination of John F. Kennedy may be less relevant than a meme of a sitting US president perhaps mired in scandal or in the spotlight due to a soundbite taken out of context. *Succinctly*, political memes and their perceived importance often follow the news cycle. This means that while particular memes as reactions to a political issue/event may be short-lived, their discursive function remains a tenable option for later use.

Spain (and Catalonia)

In October 2017, the parliament of Catalonia, a region within Spain, voted to cede from Spain and become an independent state. This action had several subsequent results both in the real world and in online spaces in the form of internet memes, video games, and even a parody nation-state with its own flag and news forum. The vote was declared illegal and former Prime Minister of Spain, Mariano Rajoy, dismissed the 130th President of Catalonia, Carles Puigdemont, forcing him to flee to Belgium for a stay in exile. Rajoy called for renewed elections in December 2017, which again resulted in a majority for independence. As of April 2018, Puigdemont was detained in Germany after attempting to return from a conference in Copenhagen, Denmark. A German court decided against extradition to Spain on the more serious charge of rebellion, and decided to permit extradition on the charge of corruption due to questions of the handling of public funds by Puigdemont. Spain has since dropped arrest warrants, but Puigdemont has chosen to return to Belgium. Unlike the previous examples included in this chapter, the Catalonian story is accompanied by a touch of levity, perhaps in part due to a sense of reality apathy, to be discussed in the section on Russia.

Spanish netizens responded to the parliamentary chaos with humorous memes and related parodies. For example, internet memes that emerged from the independence movement and votes largely portray Puigdemont as a man on the run, especially in one such parody mash-up in which Puigdemont's face is added to an image of Tom Hanks' character in the eponymous film *Forrest Gump* during his run across the USA in the film. Another related meme positions Puigdemont as *Gump* sitting on the bench from the famous film poster, holding a box of chocolates with the text "viaje a ninguna parte" (travel to nowhere).

In an image-macro Puigdemont meme, the estranged leader is shown in a dramatic yet humorous scene from *Airplane!* that depicts a fellow passenger apparently drinking gasoline. The text of the meme suggests that Puigdemont is oblivious that his actions are not as heroic as he may wish to insist. The semiotic function of the insertion of Puigdemont into a scene from a film (which is itself a satire) is for the meme to *satirize the satire*. On Twitter, the embattled Catalonian leader enjoyed no respite from critical memes. Puigdemont was remixed into a version of the so-called *Distracted Boyfriend* meme.

Figure 4.2 Distracted Boyfriend, Distracted Puigdemont.

On October 30, 2017, one twitter user posted the *Distracted Puigdemont* meme to criticize his departure from Catalonia and retreat to Belgium to escape extradition, shown in Figure 4.2. Another meme simply shows a photoshopped image of Puigdemont with an added monocle and elaborate moustache explaining that "You are wrong about my identity. My name is Charles Pauxlemaunt", with the implication again being a critique of his escape to Belgium (given the adjusted French-sounding last name), shown in Figure 4.3.

This is not to say that the discursive reactions are devoid of critique; on the contrary, the issue of Catalonian independence is a heated topic in Spain and is in and of itself also an important issue within the context of European integration – especially when one compares international reactions to the declaration of independence by Kosovo in 2008 and the same action by Catalonia in 2018.

Regardless, the international community has largely acknowledged that the Catalonian issue is an internal matter, and the question of sovereignty appears to be settled as a Spanish matter. As a result of the vote, the exile of Puigdemont, and the general sentiment in Spain on all sides of the issue, internet memes have been deployed as a form of political expression, itself representative of digital ideological practice.

«Se equivoca usted de persona. Yo me llamo Charles Pauxlemaunt.»

7:55 AM - 30 Oct 2017

4,401 Retweets **6,242** Likes

♡ 67   ⊔ 4.4K   ♡ 6.2K

Figure 4.3 Puigdemont or Pauxlemaunt?

Gamifying Political Discourse

The development of a video game by the name of *PuigdeKong* appears perhaps to be a temporary culmination of popular reaction to the independence vote and ensuing political and cultural crisis. The game itself allows the player to assume the role of Puigdemont on his embattled journey navigating a series of obstacles in the form of police, judges, and even Prime Minister Rajoy as a remixed Donkey Kong (Hipertextual Redacción, 2018). While the game is not a meme per se, it represents a ludic response from members of participatory digital culture and functions as a playful way to transcend the seriousness of the situation simultaneously by criticizing the political ramifications of the independence movement in Spain. In the words of a Catalan illustrator who assisted in *PuigdeKong*'s creation, Jordi Calvís, "[v]ideo games can be a powerful communication tool – and so can humor. Together they help us survive the sad, difficult, demoralizing reality of politics" (Frayer, 2018).

As noted previously with regard to the work of Jean Baudrillard, the video game as well as the internet memes that emerged as a response to the political unrest represent ways in which individuals make sense of a reality in which alienation encourages embrace of the hyperreal.

Baudrillard analyzed the relationship between cultural production and the ways in which individuals are informed and represented through and by television yet his perspectives also apply to this discussion, at least as a means to understand why memes as well as the *PuigdeKong* video game and other examples are important political expressions. The internet memes, video game, etc. represent expressions of an intertextual awareness of multiple forms of media as opposed to content of a message. The structure of online spaces and the media that we use to express ourselves favor succinctly articulated, truncated meaning. Internet memes are ideal for this.

The choice to gamify the Catalan independence movement as well as the internet memes suggests an "imperialism of communication", which is the act to "increase the amount of channels, opinions, voices and information irrespective of the number of people who are actually listening or engaging... [and this] upholds a principle of mediation rather than communication" (Stevenson, 2002, p. 167). The discursive practice afforded by internet memes supplants knowledge and fact with fascination and spectacle, especially in areas of political participation or malaise. While I maintain, naturally, that internet memes are discursive units of culture and are therefore communicative, I do not imply that in this example of the "imperialism of communication" an absence of communication exists. Rather, it is precisely the political upheavals that mark contemporary society in terms of fragmentation, polarization, etc. that encourage a migration away from the real toward the intertextual creation and merging of various media forms and genres in order to make sense of the world. This is perhaps especially the case with the parody nation-state *Tabarnia*.

Tabarnia: The Parody which begat the Real

In this discussion of *Tabarnia*, it is worthwhile to consider Baudrillard's relevance to the creation of a parody nation-state. A serious interpretation of Baudrillard reveals that people – weary and disillusioned by the state of the pressures and tensions saturating the real world – flee to the hyperreal world produced by mass media in order to experience life that is more real than real. I have appropriated Zizek's phrase *ideology-in-action* to suggest that behaviors, choices, desires, expressions, etc. representative of ideology are carried out as actions, hence the phrase included in this work, *ideological practice*. It bears mentioning that *Tabarnia*, as a hyperreal nation-state, demonstrates ideological practice perhaps most clearly because of its status as a fiction.

In the documentary film *The Perverts Guide to Ideology* (2012), directed by Sophie Fiennes, Zizek asserts that "the tragedy of our predicament, when we are within ideology, is that when we think that we escape it, into our dreams, at that point we are within ideology". It is within the virtual (or simulated, imagined, dreamt, etc.) that the individual is able to *realize* critique of ideology, yet that process is always already an aspect of an *ideological practice.*

With the example of *Tabarnia,* this is an intentional creation of a satirical, parody nation-state. This action, in terms of the larger discussion of internet memes within digital culture, articulates a critique of the current political events in Spain with respect to the independence movement but also with regard to the rhetoric used on both sides of that issue. The function of the *Tabarnia* parody is to allow for Spanish citizens affected by or living in areas within what is identified as Catalonia to form an autonomous region that maintains fealty to Spain. The name itself is a portmanteau of two regions within Catalonia namely Tarragona and Barcelona. Spanish politician Juan Carlos Girauta opined in a tweet that "Tabarnia is a merciless mirror for the nationalists; it's the reflection of their lack of solidarity and clumsiness" (Alandete, 2017).

What must be emphasized is the striking facet of a people feeling that only by the creation of a parody country, a fictional nation-state can political and socio-cultural critique be made possible. Thus, a fantasy produced by a discourse allows for the treatment and deliberation of the real.

Russia: Strategic Relativism and the Politics of Eternity

The first case study handles the subject of Russian interference in the 2016 US election. The rationale for this choice is, unironically, not political from my point of view. Rather, it represents the dynamic aspect of political memes: how the merging of visual-textual messages deployed for persuasive purposes appealed to a specific agenda on behalf of the Putin government. In April 2018, Mark Zuckerberg, CEO of Facebook, underwent congressional hearings about data breaches, the question of whether Facebook constitutes a monopoly, the role of *shadow profiles* (data collected from individuals who do not even have a Facebook account), and the ways in which Cambridge Analytica utilized personal data from Facebook users in order to assist in the Trump campaign for president. How does any of this connect to politics and/or Russia? As noted by historian Timothy Snyder (2018) in his book *The Road to Unfreedom: Russia, Europe, America*, "Russian platforms served content to American conspiracy sites with enormous viewership" (p. 247). A specific example is the now non-existent Facebook page *Heart of Texas* which espoused views on Texan secession from the union. Facebook has since closed approximately 500 or more pages some of which were directly managed by Russia (Bertrand, 2017; Michel, 2017).

Interference in 2016

The *Heart of Texas* Facebook page deployed internet memes aimed at specific ideological aims and was one of the many operations of the Russian-based Агентство интернет-исследований (Agenstvo internet-issledovanii), or the Internet Research Agency. In Russia, the group is based in St. Petersburg and is responsible for "thousands of fake Twitter, Facebook and other social media accounts [which] have been created in a once-secret attempt to sway public opinion against the West" (ShareAmerican/U.S. State Department, 2015). The motivation for this deployment of internet memes is related to *strategic relativism*, or the intentions to make other states weaker in order to maintain a Russian status quo (Snyder, 2018, p. 195).

In the memes created for the approximately quarter-million followers of *Heart of Texas*, there was a tendency to portray Texas as a "Christian nation", associate Hillary Clinton with Osama bin Laden, and undermine LGBT issues by rephrasing the acronym to mean "liquor, guns, bacon, and tits". In addition, the site played on tense race relations in the USA by incorporating latent and obvious racist rhetoric from the then-Trump presidential campaign. It also featured anti-immigration and anti-Islamic memes. Despite the questionable level of English in many posts (typos and poor grammar were common features of posts and memes made for *Heart of Texas*), the popularity of the site remained strong until it was taken down.

While I do not posit a causal relationship between political memes and political action, a relationship exists which suggests that the influence memes may have on human behavior is not as controversial or provocative as one might think. Well before the internet, Marshall McLuhan ruminated about the implications of technological integration and how this impacts human interaction. In what can be termed *medium theory*, McLuhan argues that "once technologies are integrated into a 'way of life', it may be difficult to be without them" (Holmes, 2005, p. 181). The connection to memes on Facebook is as follows: people can become "fascinated by any extension of themselves in any material other than themselves" (McLuhan, 1994, p. 51), and internet memes offer a tightly encapsulated way to express discursive practice efficiently and succinctly, and the ease by which memes can be further remixed and spread underscores this point. The Russian intervention in the 2016 presidential election obviously incorporated other methods than memes, but the use of memes as well as fake news suggests that people are more susceptible to suggestion than perhaps previously thought, despite having smart phones which could be used to check the validity of potentially dubious content. As followers of *Heart of Texas* encountered internet memes, reacted to them, etc., they were able to view their ideological practice as confirmed and justified.

The construction of the memes favored simple language and Texas-oriented patriotism by making appeals to its uniqueness in terms of being the only state to enter the union via treaty or that its size suggests nationhood. Through the multiple types of appeals, the intertextuality of presumed desires to secede from the union served the Russian agenda of strategic relativism to undermine the USA at a time of political upheaval.

In terms of the *Heart of Texas* and related efforts to influence public opinion in the USA ahead of the 2016 election, we again see the essence of politics of eternity as a form of ideological practice. Specifically, and also with regard to fake news stories which circulated online prior to the election, internet memes that seek to influence a person or group through the means of encouraging fear and suspicion operate on the assumption that truth is unattainable and only doubt is important because it is powerful. "A plausible future requires a factual present" (Snyder, 2018, p. 160) and if individuals are inundated with digital myths in the form of internet memes, truth is greatly at risk. By appealing to fears and anxieties, Russian memes seek to sow mistrust in the governing system of the USA by casting doubt on the assumption that the authorities serve in the interest of the common good. Such was the function of the Russian interference ahead of the 2016 presidential election in the USA.

Russia's 2018 Election: Participatory Culture or Political Malaise?

A look at Russian memes created in response to the 2018 Russian presidential election offers a slightly different perspective. In 2015, the Russian internet regulator Роскомнадзор (Rozkomnadzor) reminded users about the prohibition of "using a photo of a public figure to embody a popular internet meme which has nothing to do with the celebrity's personality" (Hamilton, 2016, p. 6). While this was reported erroneously as a general ban on internet memes in Russia, the Justice Ministry of Russia did, in fact, list the images of the so-called *Gay Clown Putin* in their *Federal List of Extremist Materials*. Despite the censorship, internet users proceeded with creating memes to voice opposition to Putin's lengthy leadership on the social media platform ВКонтакте (VKontakte), which is similar in design to Facebook and claims nearly 500 million users (VKontakte, 2018). In the lead up to and in the wake of the Russian presidential election, users posted memes to express their opinions.

One such meme, featured in Figure 4.4, actually features Putin as a cyborg with the simple caption "Elections: Year 2127". The mash-up of a real-world event with science fiction and the insertion of a simple textual message work together to deliver a searing critique of the status quo

ВЫБОРЫ 2127г.

Figure 4.4 Putin as Cyborg, *Elections: Year 2127.*

in Russia. Humor operates superficially; it is a utilitarian component which operationalizes the meme to function further as an enthymeme, or visual argument.

Another meme in a panel format shows the same image of Putin (and one image of Dmitry Medvedev) alongside text that reads "2000–2004 Putin I", "2004–2008 Putin II", "2008–2012 Pseudo-Putin" (Medvedev), "2012–2018 Putin III", and "2018–2024 Putin IV". The implication is clear. Another meme posted to Eclectic European Memes on Facebook (Figure 4.5) shows the critical perspective of women in Russian politics with Putin claiming that a woman cannot become Russia's president since he is not a woman.

An additional meme, shown in Figure 4.6, depicts a ballot on which is written "Are you not against, whether Putin becomes president?" Only two responses are possible: "Yes, I am not against" and "No, I am not against". Again, humor is deployed for the purpose of social salience, so that it enters into the discourse and is utilized as a critical expression.

Another text-based meme suggests that "the main events of 2018 – the Russian presidential election and the Olympic Games – took place without the participation of Russians". Finally, a remix of a Play Station

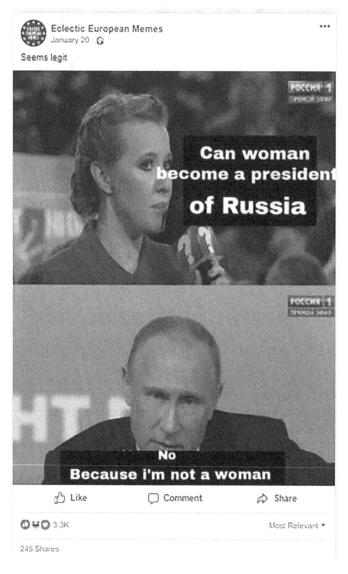

Figure 4.5 Putin is Not a Woman.

4 game *Grand Theft Auto* depicts images of Putin, related politicians, as well as the head of the Russian Orthodox Church with the textual moniker "six more years of bullshit".

The implications of these oppositional memes are two-sided. Humor may be essential in memes but certainly also functions as a semiotic

Figure 4.6 Russian Ballot Remix.

structural component. As such its function is to provoke an initial reaction, and perhaps humor may motivate others in the creation and dissemination of memes. Further, the function of the humor within the meme is a kind of *digital analgesic*: humor is necessary to advance the real substance of the meme, namely the visual argument.

Beyond humor remains a critique of the dominant system. It is at once the recognition of ideological practice and an affirmation of the inability to augment one's role within that ideology apart from perhaps spreading memes to voice some semblance of opposition. Political malaise perhaps best characterizes the internet memes deployed in opposition to Putin or at least to make the assertion that Russia is not a democracy. These memes illustrate a sentiment of something to the effect of '*the status quo is unacceptable but all we can do about it is shitpost and make memes*'. To put it more eloquently, these memes represent a visual affirmation of the *politics of eternity*. As Snyder (2018) notes the politics of eternity means,

> the same thing over and over again, a tedium exciting to believers because of the illusion that it is particularly theirs. Of course, this sense of 'us and them', or as fascists prefer, 'friends and enemies', is the least specific human experience of them all; to live within it is to sacrifice individuality.

(p. 35)

Here, Snyder is describing the state of modern Russia, that it has essentially topped-out and cannot outdo its perceived enemies so it has embraced an authoritarian, fascist type of rule but one which requires its followers to go along with it, embrace the spectacle, and acknowledge that there is no real truth, except their own lies. Within the framework of the memes described above, we see the outcome of living in a society that has no future, only a permanent and painful present, but the pain is less severe than what can be exerted on others. The ballot meme described above brilliantly captures this sentiment. Basically, it acknowledges that there is no democracy but that within the context of Putin's sovereign or managed democracy (a term introduced by Vladislav Surkov, a Russian businessman, former Deputy Chief of the Russian Presidential Administration, and current adviser to Putin), citizens are, of course, still expected to participate in the spectacle of reaffirming the state's authority. The memes demonstrate visually the outcome of a society immersed within spectacle, which is not simply an assemblage of images but *forms* the social relations among individuals and is mediated by images (Holmes, 2005, p. 32).

Comparative Analysis

To close this section on Russia, I address these two cases comparatively. On the one hand, Russian intervention in the US election took the form of deliberate coopting of Facebook pages, not to mention the approximately 50,000 Twitter accounts linked to Russian automated bots that pumped out material ahead of the 2016 election (Swaine, 2018). On the other hand, Russian social media remains an online space for individuals – ostensibly Russians expressing subversive views antithetical to the dominant governing system – to post memes that mock not a political platform or politician per se, but the immutability of their political reality.

Russia's *strategic relativism* aims to destabilize the USA through the deployment of memes on social media, in part. The lesson to be learned, regardless of whether one wishes to buy into the idea of potential Russian collusion with the Trump campaign, is that memes have ideational and persuasive value. This is also true of the memes posted in response to the 2018 Russian election; the difference is simply in the political and strategic motivation to use memes for these purposes.

Given the persuasive capacity of memes, it is worth considering the challenge posed to a knowable, objective truth in terms of the ways in which memes can apparently be used for persuasive purposes. French philosopher Jean Baudrillard offers a perplexing perspective on the question of the mass media and mass culture. While he spoke of the relationship between television in general and mediated forms of advertising, his view is equally relevant to the concerns addressed above. Baudrillard (1994) asks whether "mass media [are] on the side of power in the manipulation of the masses, or are they on the side of masses in the liquidation of meaning, in the violence perpetrated on meaning, and in fascination?" (p. 84). He is concerned about the *murder of the real* through the distribution of hyperreal forms. Baudrillard asks whether it is the "media that induce fascination in the masses, or is it the masses who direct the media into the spectacle" (p. 84)? With respect to internet memes, whether those used in the Russian interference in the US election or those used on seemingly innocuous sites such as *Classical Art Memes*, the ability to quickly remix a piece of culture into something artificial yet discernible and potentially also critical means that the hyperreality of internet memes has likely subsumed agential awareness of the origin of the real.

In other words, it is the process of memetic production (the systematic reproduction of symbols of symbols, etc.) that occurs and not meaningful civic discourse. It is especially important to consider the role of *reality apathy* with regard to the deployment of internet memes on political topics or for such purposes. Aviv Ovadya, the chief technologist at the Center for Social Media at the University of Michigan's School of Information, offers the term *reality apathy* to describe a possible reaction in people to a perceived onslaught of misinformation (Warzel, 2018). While Ovadya was primarily speaking about fake news in general, we can also apply this concept to internet memes considering the intermingling of real-world actors and imagined, conspiracy-theory, popular cultural, etc. referents. It is precisely the emergence of internet memes and their deployment in various contexts that speaks to reality apathy. In other words, people are overwhelmed with the challenges of the modern world, and they seek comfort away from political and socio-cultural alienation in online spaces.

The rapidity of sharing and curating, reacting to and liking, etc. internet memes is a substitution of community with illusory linkages to imagined groups. This rather pessimistic view I offer as a critique of internet memes and the vagaries of their deployment in an ever-increasing environment of TL; DR (too long; didn't read). However, it is also well-documented that participatory (digital) culture can achieve positive results and change (Marichal, 2013; Petray, 2013). Pragmatically, however, the presence of internet memes in online spaces as a form of communication suggests an apathetic view of reality. The motivation for this state of the internet reflects a primary desire to replace the (perceived) unfavorable reality with that which is present in a given series of internet memes, whether for political and/or strictly humorous means. Future research should explore the factors of reality apathy, strategic relativism, and the politics of eternity to discover applied uses of these concepts in mediated discourse, in memes or otherwise.

China, and the Question of Censoring Internet Memes

The choice to include a section on China is in part to acknowledge the unprecedented removal of term limits allowing current President Xi Jinping to rule indefinitely. The emphasis in this brief section is less on specific memes than on the role of censorship of internet memes and why this matters politically. As noted above, with the removal of term limits in China came a flurry of internet memes which positioned Xi Jinping in an apparent unfavorable light.

In the time since banning Winnie the Pooh, mash-ups of Xi as "Emperor Winnie" have appeared and have been removed by state censorship apparatuses. This is a resurgence of the *Winnie the Pooh-Xi Jinping* meme as it first emerged after a meeting between then US President Barack Obama and Xi in 2013. While it is unclear how or why this comparison was made, the association of the Chinese president with a cartoon character such as Winnie the Pooh appealed to Chinese netizens and incensed Chinese censors (Brimelow, 2018). In fact, even references to "Little Bear Winnie", the moniker for Winnie the Pooh in China are banned from Chinese online spaces such as Weibo, China's version of Twitter (Katz, 2017).

This section is driven by a simple question, one whose answer may at first appear to be equally simplistic. Essentially, why does the People's Republic of China care about internet memes? Why does it care so much about, for example, comparisons between Winnie the Pooh and Xi Jinping, and further, why does the choice to censor such image macro memes effectively become state policy?

Crushing Criticism or Internet Sovereignty?

An initial tempting answer might suggest that this query is futile: the reason for banning the memes is to put restraint on any criticism of the leadership. This perspective, while reductive, is at least partially correct, but only presents one perspective of the strategy of so-called *cybersovereignty*, a concept supported by Wang Huming, a former professor and current member of the seven-person Politburo Standing Committee. Basically, cybersovereignty is an official "Chinese policy term used to argue that countries should be free to control the internet within their borders, even if it means censoring" (Mozur, 2017). This may be an updated version of an earlier term known as *internet sovereignty* introduced by the Chinese government in 2010 which obligated all internet users and organizations (in and outside of China) to follow Chinese rules (China.org.cn, 2018). Regardless, a senior fellow at the Council on Foreign Relations, Elizabeth C. Economy, suggested in early 2017 that China appears somewhat schizophrenic regarding its treatment of media and its enactment of a sustainable policy. Specifically, she noted that the Chinese government understands that "[Chinese netizens] need press freedom and the information it provides, but [is] worried about opening the door to the type of freedoms that could lead to the regime's downfall" (Xu & Albert, 2017). However, to ban internet memes that fall unfavorably in the view of Chinese leadership suggests that memes inhere a discursive power.

Elevation of the Semiotic: The China Dream

The choice to ban particular memes such as the Winnie the Pooh references reflects some level of understanding of the ways participatory digital culture expresses itself. It is within the semiotic construction of the memes that this understanding takes hold: references to a culture that is perceived as external to the China Dream and using such references to critique or lampoon Chinese leadership must be expunged. The China Dream is Xi Jinping's espoused political ideology for his administration moving forward into the twenty-first century and is discussed in greater detail in a subsequent paragraph.

The expulsion of such internet memes represents a significant step toward an unprecedented control of online expression in an era of massive online participation. Indeed, China's exerted control over the internet has translated into the partial or complete blocking of several major sites such as Google, including sites connected to it such as YouTube, Gmail, Google Docs, etc., Wikipedia, Twitter, Facebook, Instagram, and many more (ViewDNSinfo, 2018). Given the participatory nature of such sites, the choice to ban them at first appears connected to a desire to avoid any and all organizing within China that could amount to demonstrations, protests, etc. which the Chinese government naturally views as a threat to its order. However, another, perhaps more practical reason for the blocking is simply to encourage Chinese cyberspace development within China for the purpose of content control but also to allow Chinese internet firms to operate without undue competition in the world's largest single online market.

According to Internet Live Stats, as of 2016 well over 720 million people in China have access to the internet, which is a 52% population penetration in China and a global penetration of around 21% of all internet users. Xi Jinping's proposed China Dream helps to explain the manner of control over the internet in China as well as why internet memes are also excluded forms of discursive practice online. The China Dream is Xi's ideological platform which emphasizes four main aspects: a strong China (in terms of politics, science, military, diplomacy, and economy); a civilized China (with respect to equity, fairness, and a high emphasis on morality); a harmonious China (amity across all social strata); and a beautiful China (in terms of lowering pollution and encouraging a healthy environment) (Kuhn, 2013). The emphases on harmony and morality are two common features to Xi's rhetoric and offer a tenable explanation as to why Chinese censors exclude the superficially mundane image-macro internet memes, such as the Winnie the Pooh references.

If You Don't Like Reality, Change It

To close this section on China, I wish to refer to line in Jean Baudrillard's (1994) *Simulacra and Simulation*. The book is his examination of the interrelationships between media and culture and the distortions and disruptions of reality as a consequence of interacting with cultural symbols mediated through various forms in the construction of a shared social and cultural experience. On the first page of his work, Baudrillard writes

> [t]oday abstraction is no longer that of the map, the double, the mirror or the concept. Simulation is no longer that of a territory, a referential being or a substance. It is the generation by models of a real without origin or reality: a hyperreal. The territory no longer precedes the map, nor survives it. Henceforth, it is the map that precedes the territory – precessions of simulacra – it is the map that engenders the territory...

Baudrillard's words are a criticism of the ways in which mediated forms of expression and representation destroy the original. The *simulacra* – copies that lack an original – is elevated to be our common form of material exchange in the recursive construction of society. It is tempting to apply this critique only to China given the details described about the manner of Chinese censorship with respect to internet memes. The blocking of sites such as Facebook and Twitter and the creation of Chinese versions represents simulacra: by destroying or removing access to the other, a simulated version is offered to Chinese netizens. But the price of admission to the sites requires strict adherence to a code of conduct and accepting that certain specific forms of expression are prohibited and will be removed. Is this not similar to the "Western" experience? Is China so unique in this regard? Is our ideological practice (by "our" I simply refer to a social and cultural position that is distinct from the Chinese experience) preventing us from seeing the corruption of reality afforded by online forms of expression such as internet memes?

I posit that Baudrillard's simulacra represents a manner of operation of the internet in that originals do not matter, and the expression of political views in the form of internet memes carries a vacuous and meaningless value without the ability or desire to enact social change in the real world. This is especially the case if civic engagement is muted, redirected, or prohibited. In China, social expressions counter to the dominant system are prohibited and political expression is strictly enforced. Little or no change other than that which is ordained by the Chinese leadership will be permitted (which is not to say that social/political change is impossible). In other contexts, such as in the earlier examples of the USA and Russia, internet memes were deployed for specific political purposes because of their discursive power to incite political participation (as in the *Heart of Texas* faux memes) or to express disagreement with the dominant order (as in the memes mocking Putin). If civic discourse is to be truncated to the internet meme – which at least in terms of Facebook pages and groups dedicated to memetic exchange appears to be the case at least partially – we can no longer speak authoritatively about truth but rather truths. The insertion of popular culture, conspiracy theories, uninformed opinion, and/or blatant racism and bigotry into internet memes and the spread of such messages online is a digital precession of simulacra.

References

Alandete, D. (2017, December 27). Tabarnia: The hoax independence movement trending now in Spain. *El Pais*. Retrieved from https://elpais.com/elpais/2017/12/27/inenglish/1514368061_809906.html

Allen, K. (2018, February 26). China censorship after Xi Jinping presidency extension proposal. *BBC News: China*. Retrieved from https://www.bbc.com/news/world-asia-china-43198404

Arestova, A. Y., Balandina, E. V., & Budko, I. A. (2015). The etymology of "Internet memes" [ЭТИМОЛОГИЯ "ИНТЕРНЕТ-МЕМОВ"]. Paper presented at the Student Science Forum 2015, Moscow, Russian Federation. Retrieved from http://www.scienceforum.ru/2015/pdf/13752.pdf

Baudrillard, J. (1994). *Simulacra and simulation* (S. F. Glaser, Trans.). Ann Arbor: University of Michigan Press.

Bertrand, N. (2017, September 17). Texas secession movement: Russia-linked Facebook group asked us to participate in anti-Clinton rallies. *Business Insider Deutschland*. Retrieved from http://www.businessinsider.de/russia-facebook-group-ads-texas-secession-secede-trump-clinton-2017-9?r=US&IR=T

Blattberg, C. (2001). Political philosophies and political ideologies. *Public Affairs Quarterly, 15*(3), 193–217. Retrieved from https://ssrn.com/abstract=1755117

Bock, M. A., & Figueroa, E. J. (2017). Faith and reason: An analysis of the homologies of black and blue lives Facebook pages. *New Media & Society*, 1–22. doi:10.1177/1461444817740822

Boynton, G. R. (2004). Legislatures. In M. Hawkesworth & M. Kogan (Eds.), *Encyclopedia of government and politics* (2nd ed., pp. 294–306). London: Routledge.

Brimelow, B. (2018, February 27). Winnie the Pooh memes are getting banned on social media after China announces Xi Jinping may stay in power for life. *Business Insider: Deutschland*. Retrieved from https://www.businessinsider.de/winnie-the-pooh-memes-china-censored-xi-jinping-2018-2?r=US&IR=T

China.org.cn (2018). Information office of the state council of the People's Republic of China. Retrieved from http://china.org.cn/government/whitepaper/node_7093508.htm

Denisova, A. (2014, December 4). *Online memes as a means of the carnivalesque resistance*. Paper presented at the symposium Politics and Humour:

Theory and Practice, Kent, UK. Retrieved from https://www.academia.edu/9865338/_2014_Online_Memes_as_Means_of_the_Carnivalesque_Resistance_in_Contemporary_Russia

Du, S. (2014). Social media and the transformation of "Chinese nationalism": "Igniting positive energy" in China since the 2012 London Olympics. *Anthropology Today, 30*(1), 5–8.

Ekdale, B., & Tully, M. (2013). Makmende Amerudi: Kenya's collective reimagining as a meme of aspiration. *Critical Studies in Media Communication, 31*(4), 283–298. doi:10.1080/15295036.2013.858823

Fiennes, S., Holly, K., Rosenbaum, M., & Wilson, J. (Producers), & Fiennes, S. (Director). (2012, September 7). *The pervert's guide to ideology* [Motion picture]. United Kingdom: Zeitgeist Films.

Frayer, L. (2018, February 1). Memes, videogames mock Catalonia's prolonged deadlock with Spain. *National Public Radio: Parallels.* Retrieved from https://www.npr.org/sections/parallels/2018/02/01/582215221/memes-video-games-mock-catalonias-prolonged-deadlock-with-spain

Giddens, A. (1984). *The constitution of society: Outline of the theory of structure.* Berkeley: University of California Press.

Hamilton, C. (2016). World politics 2.0: An introduction. In C. Hamilton & L. J. Shepard (Eds.), *Understanding popular culture and world politics in the digital age* (pp. 3–13). New York: Routledge.

Hechtkopf, K. (2009, August 18). Artist behind "Joker" image revealed. *CBS News.* Retrieved from https://www.cbsnews.com/news/artist-behind-obama-joker-picture-revealed/

Hipertextual Redacción (2018, January 29). PuigdeKong, the 'indepe[ndence]' game for the investiture of Puigdemont [PuigdeKong, el 'juego indepe' para la investidura de Puigdemont]. Retrieved from https://hipertextual.com/juno/investidura-puigdemont-puigdekong

Holmes, D. (2005). *Communication theory: Media, technology and society.* Thousand Oaks, CA: Sage.

Jenkins, H., Ford, S., & Green, J. (2013). *Spreadable media.* New York: New York University Press.

Katz, B. (2017, July 17). Why censors are targeting Winnie-the-Pooh in China. *Smithsonian.com.* Retrieved from https://www.smithsonianmag.com/smart-news/why-censors-are-targeting-winnie-the-pooh-china-180964075/

Kennicott, P. (2009, August 6). Obama as the Joker betrays racial ugliness, fears. *Washington Post.* Retrieved from http://www.washingtonpost.com/wp-dyn/content/article/2009/08/05/AR2009080503876.html??noredirect=on

El Khachab, C. (2016). Living in darkness: Internet humor and the politics of Egypt's electricity infrastructure. *Anthropology Today, 32*(4), 21–24.

Kligler-Vilenchik, N., & Thorson, K. (2015). Good citizenship as a frame contest: Kony2012, memes, and critiques of the networked citizen. *New Media & Society, 8*(9), 1–19. doi:10.1177/1461444815575311

Kuhn, R. L. (2013, June 4). Xi Jinping's Chinese dream. *The New York Times.* Retrieved from https://www.nytimes.com/2013/06/05/opinion/global/xi-jinpings-chinese-dream.html

Marichal, J. (2013). Political Facebook groups: Micro-activism and the digital front stage. *First Monday, 18*, Article 12.

McLuhan, M. (1994). *Understanding media* (Reprint ed.). MIT Press.

Michel, C. (2017, October 17). How the Russians pretended to be Texans – and Texans believed them. *The Washington Post*. Retrieved from https://www.washingtonpost.com/news/democracy-post/wp/2017/10/17/how-the-russians-pretended-to-be-texans-and-texans-believed-them/?noredirect=on&utm_term=.59732d0cf018

Milian, M. (2009, Aug 17). Obama joker artist unmasked: A fellow Chicagoan. *Los Angeles Times: Political Commentary*. Retrieved from http://latimesblogs.latimes.com/washington/2009/08/obama-joker-artist.html

Mozur, P. (2017, December 3). China's top ideologue calls for tight control of internet. *The New York Times: Asia*. Retrieved from https://www.nytimes.com/2017/12/03/world/asia/china-internet-censorship-wang-huning.html

Pearce, K. E., & Hajizada, A. (2014). No laughing matter: Humor as a means of dissent in the digital era: The case of authoritarian Azerbaijan. *Demokratizatsiya, 22*, 67–85. Retrieved from https://www.gwu.edu/~ieresgwu/assets/docs/demokratizatsiya%20archive/GWASHU_DEMO_22_1/B158221228502786/B158221228502786.pdf

Petray, T. (2013). Self-writing a movement and contesting Indigeneity: Being an aboriginal activist on social media. *Global Media Journal: Australian Edition, 7*(1), 1–20.

Phillips, W. (2009, August 14). "Why so socialist?" Unmasking the joker [Web log comment]. Retrieved from http://henryjenkins.org/blog/2009/08/unmasking_the_joker.html

Oppenheim, M. (2017, February 23). Donald Trump still calls Alex Jones for advice, claims the InfoWars founder and far right conspiracy theorist. *The Independent*. Retrieved from http://www.independent.co.uk/news/world/americas/donald-trump-alex-jones-calls-phone-advice-infowars-conspiracy-theorist-far-right-sandy-hook-a7595136.html

Saito, A. P. (2017). *Moe* and internet memes: The resistance and accommodation of Japanese popular culture in China. *Cultural Studies Review, 23*(1), 136–150. doi: 10.5130/csr.v23i1.5499

ShareAmerican/U.S. State Department (2015, November 4). Everything you wanted to know about trolls but were afraid to ask. *Share America*. Retrieved from https://share.america.gov/trolls-everything-you-wanted-to-know/

Shifman, L. (2014). *Memes in digital culture*. Cambridge: MIT Press.

Snyder, T. (2018). *The road to unfreedom: Russia, Europe, America*. London: Penguin Random House.

Statista (2018). Number of monthly active Facebook users worldwide as of 1st quarter 2018 (in millions). Retrieved from https://www.statista.com/statistics/264810/number-of-monthly-active-facebook-users-worldwide/

Stevenson, N. (2002). *Understanding media cultures* (2nd ed.). Thousand Oaks, CA: Sage.

Swaine, J. (2018, January 20). Twitter admits far more Russian bots posted on election than it had disclosed. *The Guardian: Tech*. Retrieved from https://www.theguardian.com/technology/2018/jan/19/twitter-admits-far-more-russian-bots-posted-on-election-than-it-had-disclosed

ViewDNSinfo (2018). Retrieved from http://www.viewdns.info/

Vkontakte (2018). *Vkontake's user catalog*. [Каталог пользователей ВКонтакте]. Retrieved from https://vk.com/catalog.php

Wallis, C. (2011). New media practices in China: Youth patterns, processes, and politics. *International Journal of Communication, 5*, 406–436. Retrieved from http://ijoc.org/index.php/ijoc/article/viewFile/698/530

Warzel, C. (2018, February 12). He predicted the 2016 fake news crisis. Now he's worried about an information apocalypse. *BuzzfeedNews*. Retrieved from https://www.buzzfeed.com/charliewarzel/the-terrifying-future-of-fake-news?utm_term=.lsrmKLzkY#.gmDE2Px6a

Wei, W. (2017). Good gay buddies for lifetime: Homosexually themed discourse and the construction of heteromasculinity among Chinese urban youth. *Journal of Homosexuality, 64*(12), 1667–1683, doi:10.1080/00918369.2016.1253393

Wiggins, B. E. (2014, September 22). How the Russia–Ukraine crisis became a magnet for memes. *The Conversation*. Retrieved from https://theconversation.com/how-the-russia-ukraine-crisis-became-a-magnet-for-memes-31199

Wiggins, B. E. (2016). Crimea river: Directionality in memes from the Russia-Ukraine conflict. *International Journal of Communication, 10*(2016), 451–495.

Wiggins, B. E. (2017). Digital dispatches from the 2016 US election: Popular culture, intertextuality and media power. *International Journal of Media & Cultural Politics, 13*(1–2), 197–205.

Xu, B., & Albert, E. (2017, February 17). Media censorship in China. *Council on Foreign Relations: Backgrounder*. Retrieved from https://www.cfr.org/backgrounder/media-censorship-china

5 Commercially Motivated Strategic Messaging and Internet Memes

The orientation of this chapter is that internet memes are a (potentially) powerful tactic to be used in strategic messaging despite appearing upon first glance as silly and dismissible. Several cases involving internet memes reveal both the incorporation of the internet meme as well as the Dawkinsian variant, as discussed in the first chapter. I draw distinctions, where applicable and relevant, between the *meme* as articulated by Dawkins' *mimema* (imitated thing) and *enthymeme*, understood as a visual argument whose comprehension is contingent upon the reader or viewer to fill in unspecified or omitted information. The cases derive from instances where a company paid for and/or secured the rights for using a meme as part of a commercially motivated strategic message. The chapter begins with the role of copyright and internet memes emphasizing the distinction between *communicative* and *commercial* speech.

To open this chapter, I briefly review a legal case between actor Dustin Hoffman and ABC, Inc. (formerly Capital Cities/ABC, Inc.), owned by the Walt Disney Company. This case demonstrates the structural aspects of internet memes in contemporary times despite the case not being an explicit example of an actual internet meme. Further, and connected to the cases covered in this chapter, the question of copyright as related to the production and sharing of internet memes figures prominently in this chapter primarily due to the legal implications with regard to *commercial* versus *communicative* speech.

Commercial Usage of Memes and Copyright

In 1997, the Los Angeles Magazine published an article in its March issue called *Grand Illusions*, which featured a series of digitally altered photographs of celebrities for the purpose of showing the latest fashion choices of the season. Incidentally, the article also included a guide for shopping which had information on the prices of the garments depicted in the photographs as well as locations where they could be purchased. This is a really important point, and it is connected to the legal aspect for the larger discussion of copyright and internet memes, but I will return to it momentarily. The editorial staff decided to digitally alter (in modern parlance, *remix*) a photograph of Dustin Hoffman taken from the 1982 film *Tootsie*. In the original photo from the film, the actor is shown in a glittery red evening dress, wearing high heels, and positioned in front of the flag of the USA.

In the remixed version, only Dustin Hoffman's head as the character *Tootsie* remains. Since the Los Angeles Magazine had not gained Hoffman's permission to use his visage in the printed publication, the actor filed suit on the basis of a misappropriation of "Hoffman's identity in violation of: (1) the California common law and statutory right of publicity; (2) the California unfair competition statute, Business and Professions Code § 17200; and (3) the federal Lanham Act, 15 U.S.C. § 1125(a)" (Ho, 2002, p. 534). During a first trial in a district court, the ruling held that the use of Hoffman's identity was indeed commercial speech, which enjoys less protection under the First Amendment in the Constitution of the USA on the matter of free speech. The ruling also stipulated that despite Los Angeles Magazine's claim that the use of Hoffman in the article was editorial, therefore falling under the category of communicative speech, there was no discernible relationship between a supposed editorial message and Hoffman's identity. As noted earlier, the shopping guide included in the magazine weakened the argument that the photo served a purely communicative (editorial in this sense) and not a commercial function.

However, the US Court of Appeals' Ninth Circuit overturned the ruling of the district court. Interestingly, and here we begin to see peculiar parallels to internet memes, "the court saw the article as a combination of fashion photography, humor, and visual and verbal editorial comment on classic films and famous actors" (Ho, 2002, p. 534). Essentially, the decision to take available content, namely the screen still of Dustin Hoffman as the character *Tootsie* and use computer software to digitally alter the image for a communicative purpose, is structurally identical to the manner by which individuals produce internet memes. Also, it is worth noting that the altered image possessed an additional function as a visual argument (enthymeme) in its invitation to the viewer to fill in absent information (i.e. to consider the clothing depicted; to think about the film *Tootsie* and how it compares to the times of the late 1990s, etc.).

The ruling of the US Court of Appeals centered on a perspective of speech which is understood rather rigidly as being either communicative or commercial. The main distinction between the two types of speech lies in the degree of proposing a commercial transaction. If an expression, statement, message, etc. proposes a transaction, this act is viewed as commercial speech and "is entitled to little constitutional protection" (Ho, 2002, p. 531). This differs from communicative speech which enjoys vast protections thus emboldening expressions indicative of social, cultural, political, literary, ethical, economic, artistic, and other matters. Furthermore, following the outcome of a case between Kasky v.

Nike, Inc., the California Supreme Court developed a test for determining whether a speech act falls under the commercial or communicative category. Namely, the test "requires consideration of three elements: the speaker, the intended audience, and the content of the message" (Rocha, 2017, p. 39). Additionally, the question of whether commercial interests may use internet memes as do non-commercial interests appears to hinge on the discursive aspect of the given message. Ho (2002, p. 532) also mentions that despite this apparently dichotomous relationship of *communicative* versus *commercial,* some speech acts fall into a *mixed* category involving aspects of both. Resolving this issue, at least in the courts, necessitates taking one of two approaches.

A *case-by-case* approach follows from the view that some works may be *transformative,* meaning that something new has been added to the content thus extending or developing further the purpose and meaning of the content (Ho, 2002; Rocha, 2017). This differs from a *hard-line* or *predictable line* approach, which results in the creation of a maxim by which all cases are judged regardless of other variables. Ho (2002, p. 533) astutely summarizes the advantages and disadvantages of both by stating that the "former sacrifices predictability for accuracy, while the latter sacrifices flexibility for consistency". Taken together, these perspectives of copyright with respect to the type of speech act encapsulated in a given message complicate the place of internet memes especially if a company were to share a meme as is commonplace on social media.

The Hoffman case demonstrates that the use of available content repurposed for a communicative act resulted in a lawsuit favoring the publisher. Yet, the question of whether the use of available (or spreadable) media repurposed in memes is permissible under the *Fair Use* provision of copyright is unclear (at least with regard to the USA; in the UK such a provision is known as *Fair Dealing*). As noted, the purpose of a communicative expression can be political, social, cultural, etc. and still enjoy the protections for free speech. Further, given my argument that memes inhere a discursive power indicative of ideological practice, this would seem to support the notion that internet memes are communicative, regardless of the constitutive components.

Digital culture often operates on an assumption that is unique to its essence but dissonant with respect to real-world law and practice. This assumption posits that what is available or searchable is equally useable, remixable, etc. In other words, if I can access it, I can use it, drag it off the website, download the video, remix it, etc. in order to offer my own version of whatever it happens to be. By and large, this approach largely defines much of digital culture in terms of common practice. Yet, laws remain in place despite the grab-and-share, copy/paste, etc. aspect of digital culture. As an applied example, I will distinguish between two cases. The first pertains to the so-called *Socially Awkward Penguin,* which features a photograph of a real penguin in an amusing position and as an image-macro meme, normally with top-and-bottom text with the punchline at the bottom. However, the image of the penguin is actually the intellectual property of National Geographic and is licensed through Getty Images. The meme was posted in 2015 by a nondescript German blogging group called Geek Sisters, which is non-commercial in nature, but is owned by a for-profit retail company called getDigital. Getty Images issued a missive to the parent company suggesting that if they do not receive compensation for the misuse of the penguin image, the company would pursue legal options. Approximately $900 later and the case was closed (Dewey, 2015). This contrasts from a case involving the fast-food chain Wendy's and their exemplary use of social media to connect and interact with everyday people on Twitter (Rocha, 2017).

The fast-food chain responded to a tweet inquiring whether it had any memes by posting a remix of the *Pepe the Frog* internet meme. Likely unbeknownst to Wendy's, the *Pepe the Frog* meme had already developed into a signature image of the alt-right and white supremacist movements, according to the Southern Poverty Law Center (Morlin, 2016). While it is debatable as to whether Wendy's deployed the meme for commercial purposes, the company was quick to delete the tweet and then issued an apology. However, the action taken by Wendy's, namely, the deletion of the tweet, likely occurred due to concerns about the meme's connotations adding a negative value to its brand. Regardless, no claims of copyright infringement were made.

In both instances, the action taken on social media served a communicative function; however, in regard to the Getty Images case involving the image of the penguin the main problem was the use of proprietary content without permission despite being a purely communicative act. In Wendy's case, the tweet served to connect with their Twitter followers. Further, such a move could be construed as a commercial transaction by associating digital savviness with their brand, thus increasing chances of interest in their products. In any case, future examples will likely need to determine whether it is a matter of communicative or commercial speech unless laws are adjusted. The following section explores the issue of virality with respect to commercially motivated strategic messaging.

Viral, by Design?

The success of a viral campaign is defined as producing an effect on social relations resulting in a change to cultural vocabulary, such as a catchphrase, gesture, etc. This is distinct from viral media, which though of course thematically related, can achieve viral status without the *design* required by a promotional campaign. In other words, the successful *Old Spice* commercial, for example, arguably achieved virality due to its design, whereas one person's tweet can go viral due not to the person's intention, but rather active networks (Nahon & Hemsley, 2013).

The infamous (and if not also regrettable) case of Justine Sacco's tweet from December 20, 2012 illustrates this point. The tweet, "Going to Africa. Hope I don't get AIDS. Just kidding. I'm white!", was apparently her attempt to joke sardonically about white privilege but while she only had 170 Twitter followers, it was the larger network, the followers of followers, so to speak, who picked up the tweet and made it a trending topic during her 11-hour flight to South Africa. Media can go viral by accident as well as by design. The relation to that issue with regard to commercially motivated strategic messaging is the delicate balance between design and happenstance alongside a measured awareness of risk.

For example, an advice article posted on the self-proclaimed "world's leading social intelligence company" Brandwatch argues that in order to work with memes effectively in marketing and brand conscious initiatives, it is imperative to adhere to a series of principles. According to the article, when working to make a meme function properly, that is, to make it go viral, one must consider the following conditions: the meme must be (1) easy to create; (2) easy to consume; (3) relatable to your audience; (4) shareable; (5) familiar; and (6) funny, witty, clever, or smart. For a thematic range of advice, the article opines that the following topics are good choices to consider to maximize the content's virality: (1) animals saying human things; (2) babies saying or doing adult things; (3) sayings from popular television shows or movies; (4) popular images of characters from television shows or movies; (5) popular or classic quotes; (6) puns or joke punch lines; (7) that moment when...; (8) reference the *Grumpy cat* meme; (9) reference the *Most Interesting Man in the World* meme. My point is not to levy criticism on Brandwatch as a company. To be honest, their points capture important aspects from a reverse-engineered perspective, similar to the work done by Jonah Berger in his 2016 book entitled *Contagious: Why Things Catch On*.

The misfortune in the reverse-engineered approach lies in the critical reading of viral media, internet memes, etc., unpacking the attributes and presenting these as the ingredients for copying the success. When a piece of mediated content, such as the original source video of Gary Brolsma's *Numa Numa* dance or Paul Vasquez's *Double Rainbow*, is remixed into an internet meme, parody operates as the chief storytelling device.

In other instances, such as the *Trump Executive Order* meme or the various anti-European Union memes that emerged from the Russian annexation of Crimea in 2014 (Wiggins, 2016), wherein references are made to popular culture, a comparison between a real-world actor or event and a fictional antecedent is made such as in the case of metaphor. Thus, commercially motivated strategic messages which are designed to have the look and feel of an internet meme should not underestimate the value of metaphoric references to capture the intended effect (likely a version of *jouissance*) on their (imagined) audience.

According to Umberto Eco (1984), metaphor allows us to know more about the inserted items of knowledge than the schematic relation that is constructed through metaphors, suggesting "metaphorical knowledge is knowledge of the dynamics of the real" (p. 102). While memes have a form, understanding them depends upon known referential points of fact, narrative, philosophy, etc. In other words, one must know the referent to understand the point that the meme attempts to argue, communicate, or pose. Listing the key reverse-engineered attributes of memes means that for something to "be a meme", all that is required is the tactical insertion of key points. This approach avoids the chance to *be original* and prevents such an attempt at *making a meme* to evolve through agency consonant with the vagaries of participatory digital culture. Eco's semiotics, when applied to internet memes, suggests that memes as metaphors signify structural attributes that make them seem like an internet meme, in a manufactured manner. The ease by which organizations can employ memes according to the principles advised above translates into activities that simply issue greater demand on attention first and foremost. Before proceeding with the cases, it is worthwhile first to examine a pre-digital version of media virality.

Where's the Beef? Wendy's Commercial as an Early Example of Viral Media

In 1984, Wendy's, a US fast food chain, attempted to challenge its primary competitors, namely McDonald's and Burger King, by producing a commercial in which two elderly ladies comment on the size and apparent fluffiness of a hamburger bun and are then interrupted by a third lady who interjected the famous catchphrase, *Where's the Beef?*. Clara Peller, then 80 years old, uttered the phrase, which translated into cultural capital: t-shirts, bumper stickers, Frisbees, and even a board game (Museum of Play, 2018) were produced to maximize the effect of the entrance of *Where's the Beef?* into cultural vocabulary (Nemetz, 2014).

The point of including the *Where's the Beef?* commercial and its ensuing entrance into cultural vocabulary into this discussion is fundamental to understanding the differences, as described in Chapter 1, between *meme* and *internet meme*. *Where's the Beef?* signals a true example of a Dawkinsian meme: as a catchphrase, an idea, it spread virally, well before the internet, and became commodified through marketed products but underwent no discernible change, remix, or parody as is essential for internet memes. It is true that its marketed form in terms of bumper stickers or board games suggests a change or modification of the original idea. However, the *Where's the Beef?* (Dawkinsian) meme illustrates the capacity for a single term to be shared, spread, said and repeated, for a laugh and for the need to appear salient and socially current during the time of its spread. When *Where's the Beef?* is compared to internet memes, a clear distinction emerges between *mimema* and *enthymeme*, that is, the difference between an imitated thing and a visual argument.

As discussed in Chapter 3, the Dos Equis beer commercial featuring *The Most Interesting Man in the World* introduced his catchphrase '*I don't always X, but when I do, I Y*'. In comparison with the *Where's the Beef?* (Dawkinsian) meme, the Dos Equis example became an internet meme only after consistent change, parody, iterative remixing, etc. by individuals. The catchphrase changed often for humorous effect, such as "I don't always take out the recycling, but when I do, I look like a raging alcoholic". Here, we have an example of two catchphrases, one frozen in time but relevant or remembered depending on one's knowledge of the original event (the Wendy's *Where's the Beef?* commercial), and one whose preferred or intended meaning changed depending on user-generated context. Further, the Dos Equis example changed also depending on specific semiotic choices introduced by agents acting within a specific social system in an effort to communicate something, be it mundane or profound, about society, culture, politics, etc.

A more recent example illustrates the ways in which companies actively leverage internet memes in public relations, marketing, and advertising campaigns. The relationship between the *Where's the Beef?* example and the ones to follow lies in the design of a campaign to achieve some degree of viral status. When a campaign incorporates internet memes, the purpose of such a design choice has a larger meaning, but is also potentially affected by risk, as will be shown in the cases to follow. However, the use of memes outside their (normal) digital habitat translates into an incidental benefit: appearing socially salient using internet memes means being *cool*.

The Role of *Cool* in Strategic Uses of Internet Memes

In March 2017, luxury fashion brand Gucci introduced the #TFWGucci campaign, or "that feel(ing) when Gucci", ostensibly to innovate outreach to consumers by incorporating internet memes in their attempt to promote their products. Several examples the campaign used include captioning classic art in order to provide a distanced ironic feeling about mundane situations, such as '*that feeling when*' you receive a gift that fails to meet expectations (thus implying the utility of Gucci's products as a way to re-capture what was lost). Semiotically, this occurs through visual argument. The viewer is left to fill in the intended meaning in order to connect the inserted text with the image and the implied sentiment. Similarly, the group chat and instant messaging start-up HipChat used the *Y U No...?* internet meme in a billboard campaign.

While Gucci is an established luxury brand, its deployment of memes in a luxury campaign did not have the same kind of reception as compared to the HipChat *billboard-meets-internet meme*. The HipChat campaign "was well received because the brand was an upstart trying to disrupt an established market. Edgy humor is more authentic when brands can claim a truly disruptive message" (McCrae, 2017, para. 6). Regardless of the success of either campaign, the choice to use internet memes in commercially motivated strategic messaging demonstrates that internet memes have a social salience which resonates with audiences. This is especially the case when internet memes are deployed but also *received* proportionate to the anticipated expectations from the standpoint of the company or organization. Put another way, using internet memes in advertisements, for example, exhibits the *semiotics of cool*.

Pountain and Robins (2000, p. 17–18) explain that to understand exactly what *cool* is in terms of a denotative definition, they suggest we,

> …approach by simply accepting Cool as a phenomenon that we can recognize when we see it, from its effects in human behaviour and cultural artefacts – in speech and dance, films and television shows, books and magazines, music, clothes … It doesn't take too much investigation to understand that Cool is not something that inheres in these artefacts themselves, but rather in people's attitude to them.

Thus, *cool* is clearly a concept that can be incorporated into a marketing or advertising campaign, for example, but similar to the enthymeme, it depends on a person to fill in the blanks, that is, to acknowledge a thing as *cool*. When internet memes are properly deployed, a part of the message they transmit is awareness of their function as a form of communication in popular culture, whether online or off. HipChat's use of the *Y U No..?* internet meme in a physical billboard campaign underscores the desire to appeal to a sentiment of *cool* in an attempt to bring attention to its brand. Many other examples exist, such as the remixing of the Old Spice viral video for a trailer of *Puss in Boots*. Another example comes from a US restaurant chain, Denny's, which leverages a variety of social media platforms for reaching its audiences in new and unexpected ways.

In March 2017, Denny's tweeted an image of buttermilk pancakes as maple syrup pours on a dollop of butter and flows downward on the pancake stack. The incorporation of an already-existing sub-genre of internet meme, the zoom in photo, represents an innovative form of remix by a for-profit company seeking to connect with members of participatory digital culture. Denny's tweet garnered over 120,000 retweets and 170,000 likes (Rath, 2017). Hidden messages are written within parts of the image, such as "look at the lower left corner", "now look at the lower right corner", "now look at the upper left corner", "now look in the butter", followed by the punchline, "has this distracted you from overwhelming existential dread lol" (Denny's Tumblr, 2016). However, another clever aspect of Denny's strategy was the use of memetic characteristics as opposed to an actual internet meme (whose commercial use would likely not fall under the protections of Fair Use).

The introduction of internet memes in arenas such as promotional videos, marketing, advertising, etc. suggests a purposeful deployment of internet memes given their resonance with consumers. Perhaps, the internet meme's best attribute in this regard is the ability to gain the attention of individuals and consumers alike. Its truncated form of communication grabs attention also by relying on humor. In terms of a semiotics of cool, in order to successfully use internet memes in strategic messaging, a certain degree of risk is required.

Mistakes can be made when a company generalizes an audience as a homologous mass. For example, as shown in Figure 5.1, the US Department of Health and Human Services tweeted visual information about

Figure 5.1 US Department of Health and Human Services: *Doge* Fail.

the website for healthcare.gov in the form of a *Doge* meme and did not do well with audiences. In terms of engagement, it only garnered 1,166 retweets and much of the comments express strong rejection toward the use of a *dead* meme.

Semiotically, if a company or organization wants to incorporate an internet meme in a message to its constituents, it must consider that the *use of the internet meme itself* may communicate more about how the company views *consumers* in general and demonstrates a level of awareness about internet users based, at least in part, on assumptions. If a company or organization wishes to reach out to its constituents through the deployment of memes, it should consider seriously that such a choice is itself also an act of communication. As such, it will be received and interpreted perhaps well within or beyond the intended purpose of the message. The following case studies reveal documented ways in which internet memes were used in specific public relations, marketing, or advertising campaigns.

Numa Numa Guy and the Geico Lizard

On December 6, 2004, amateur videographer Gary Brolsma uploaded a lip-synched performance of the song "Dragostea din tei" by the Moldovan boy band O-Zone. The video's first appearance on the entertainment, social media website, and flash hosting service Newgrounds. com precipitated 15.8 million views and over 2,000 pages of comments. YouTube user xloserkidx uploaded a copy of the video on August 14, 2006 and has gained over 52 million views as of October 25, 2013 (Knowyourmeme.com, 2013). Incidentally, the YouTube clip has over 321,000 likes and over 24,000 thumbs-down. As noted on the meme documentation website Knowyourmeme.com (2013),

> Dragostea din tei" (roughly translated as "Love in the Linden Tree") is a 2003 dance single by the Moldovan pop trio O-Zone. Its nickname "Numa Numa" comes from the song's Romanian lyrics "nu mă, nu mă iei" which translates to "you don't want, don't want to take me".

Numerous iterations and remixes of Brolsma's video emerged as a result of the popularity surrounding his original remix of O-Zone's song. In fact, in 2009, Brolsma partnered with Geico Insurance to make another Numa Numa video which featured the Geico gecko dancing under a lamp in the background. Various YouTube remixes of Brolsma's video as well as remixes of O-Zone's song have appeared on the video-sharing site in subsequent years. For clarity, it is important to differentiate between the initial video and the function of the iterations as an actual internet meme. The initial video is an example of a viral video, while its parodied iterations are internet memes. Thus, the function of the source, or original video, is to be a kind of springboard, a digital launching point for others to take part in the discourse, be it silly and whimsical or serious and critical. But what happens when the source video or similar content is used as a memetic template for commercial gain? Is it clever marketing or strategic deployment of cool media messages, or both?

In Brolsma's case, Geico put him in a physical setting similar to the original *Numa Numa* video but with the addition of the Geico gecko dancing in the background in a glass aquarium. According to then vice-president of marketing, Ted Ward, "[t]he gecko and some of our other icons have a passionate fan base and we think people will appreciate the 'surprise' of seeing them pop up in unexpected places. No call to action, no website address or 1–800 number, just a bit of entertainment courtesy of GEICO" (Frommer, 2009, para. 3). The choice of placing Brolsma with a sly insertion of the Geico gecko suggests two outcomes.

First, it positions Geico as *cool* given its awareness of the function of the meme as a way to potentially reach consumers. In other words, the initial choice to use the Numa Numa guy in an intertextually designed Geico commercial (with the furtive placement of the Geico gecko) is to provide individuals with something unusual, not mainstream (and therefore ideally cool) in order to resonate with (possibly millennial) audiences. Jenkins, Ford, and Green (2013) argued that when companies such as Harley Davidson, Apple, or John Deere deploy messages tailored for the individuals who are already fans or enthusiastic consumers, they are actually tapping into a commercial culture that existed before their messaging attempts were made. Similar to Gee's (2004) concept of *affinity spaces*, or online spaces where individuals share information and build up stores of knowledge, the use of Brolsma and the Geico gecko is a strategic exercise that acknowledges the power of new media messages such as internet memes.

Second, the utility of structuring the video to make it seem cool suggests an attempt to incorporate social currency in its design. While the Geico Numa Numa pairing is from 2009, the increase on figuring out new ways to get and maintain attention has not abated. Social currency as a concept suggests that if knowing about a thing has the potential to ameliorate your self-esteem, make you think you are more attractive or cool, or simply just make you feel good, then it is more likely that you will talk about, curate (Pflaeging, 2015), or share the information online (Berger, 2016). These two outcomes suggest that the Numa Numa Geico pairing is both clever marketing and simultaneously a deliberate act to seem cool (with the assumed or implied expectation of commercial gain).

Virgin Media, Vitamin Water, and the Success Kid

On August 26, 2007, photographer Laney Griner captured an image of her 11-month-old son Sammy and posted the image to her Flickr account. Since its initial upload, the image has evolved into a popular internet meme commonly referred to as the *Success Kid* meme. Technically, this particular type of meme is best called an *image macro meme*, which as described in Chapter 3 normally features an image with text either above or below but often both above and below the image. The *Success Kid* meme has evolved into a commonly used visual expression of success, winning, or simply to acknowledge that the odds were in your favor regarding a particular instance.

Initially, however, users deployed the image macro to imply frustration or anger toward someone. Sometimes it is referred to as "I hate sandcastles" given that the location of the image is a beach or "Ima fuck you up" due to the type of facial expression in the image (Knowyourmeme.com, 2010). Overtime users tended to deploy the meme to celebrate successes. In early 2012, Virgin Media compensated Griner for the use of the image in an advertising campaign often with a phrase similar to "Tim just realized his parents get **HD channels at no extra cost**". The words in bold also appeared so in the advertisements and semiotically match the intentional meaning of the *Success Kid* meme given the realization for a positive gain at no perceivable loss. This example also demonstrates an elaboration of the concept of intertextuality.

As I have noted, it is helpful to view all texts as intertexts given the unavoidable nature of incorporating meaning or reference which is not unique to a given text. The use of the *Success Kid* meme in a Virgin Media advertisement represents the affordances of digital interdiscursivity: as intertext in this example, the meme references digital culture in a static, offline billboard advertisement, similar to the *Y U No* meme mentioned earlier in its use in a similar campaign by HipChat.

In a related use of the same image, Vitamin Water obtained permission to use it for a television commercial in which a young man passes by several internet meme references, such as the *Success Kid* (as well as the *Limecat* meme which portrays a cat with a carved-out lime or small watermelon affixed to its head like a helmet). In both cases, one or several internet memes were deployed as part of a commercially driven campaign. To leverage an internet meme as part of a commercial endeavor suggests that advertisers and marketers are conscious of the salience of internet memes and seek to position themselves, their products or services as consonant with digital trends in an effort to appear current.

Delta Airline's *Internetest* Safety Video

In 2015, Delta Airlines introduced a new in-flight safety video featuring references as well as cameos of individuals and digital media content from videos that have experienced some degree of virality but have also been remixed as internet memes (Coldwell, 2015). For example, Paul Vasquez, also known by his YouTube user name hungrybear9562 or perhaps more commonly as the *Double Rainbow Guy* appeared in the video stowing away a pair of rainbows. Similar to the case of Gary Brolsma, Vasquez is the source of the internet meme but not an actual internet meme himself neither is the pair of rainbows.

During a sequence of the safety video on how to use the seatbelt appropriately, the gentleman performing the task gestures and moves his body similar to the manner made popular by South Korean pop singer, Psy in the viral video phenomenon *Gangnam Style*, a video with nearly three billion views as of this writing.

In both instances, a semiotic transference of referentiality occurs in the deployment of '*viral videos gone meme*' for the purpose of resonating with the audience and attempting to be *remark*able, as noted by Nahon and Hemsley (2013). For a video or related media content to attain virality, regardless of any discussion of internet memes, it is helpful for the content to be remarkable, meaning that the content should literally be of such a quality that individuals consuming it wish to remark about it. The remarkable quality of the Delta Airlines safety video is not its inclusion of internet memes, be they actual internet memes or references to viral videos, etc. What is really being featured in the video is an attempt by a multibillion-dollar company with over 80,000 employees to praise the wonders of the internet. Ironically, in order to resonate with audiences, the choice must be to infuse references to humorous quiddities such as the *Doge* meme or the *Annoying Orange* meme as opposed to incorporating the knowledge-based benefits of the internet.

The Delta Airlines safety video is an attempt not to employ memes per se, but rather to appeal to the structural components that are familiar, allowing memory traces (Giddens, 1984) to help us remember and relate to contextualized and inferred meaning for the purpose of a laugh, a share, a comment, or further remix. With the safety video, no new meme is created or curated; rather, its success (at being unusual, unique, or an original, etc.) lies within its design.

Concluding Discussion

Regardless of the legal implications of posting a meme for commercial purposes, what appears to be an important conclusion is actually a link to what I have discussed earlier as the *semiotics of cool*. With respect to copyright issues or concerns, the choice to deploy an internet meme by a company is, at least generally speaking, an "ill-conceived notion that their meme share will be protected by fair use" (Rocha, 2017, p. 44). However, an alternative view suggests that internet memes "are worthy of the judicial protection because they effectuate cultural interchange and the productive use of copyright, and because protecting memes responds to a market failure – that is, the inability for memes to develop without copyright infringement" (Patel, 2013, p. 256). Furthermore, the question as to whether a given speech act is communicative or commercial in nature is a matter for legal entities to pursue. However, the actual point of such use, whether purely commercial or possibly a mix of both, should be viewed as an attempt to reach out to people and to appear socially relevant and cool. The *semiotics of cool* involves some degree of risk, as noted above but also with regard to the potential legal implications of using spreadable media repurposed as a meme for commercial purposes. As in the case of the *#TFWGucci* campaign, the *semiotics of cool* suggest that the risk of using memes can backfire especially if an organization does not realize the implications of its actions. The *semiotics of cool* is a largely structural concept, rooted in the idea that an already existing entity, for example a for-profit business, can deploy an already existing meme or at least memetic playfulness (as in the example of *Denny's* earlier in the chapter) but that these actions inhere risk. Specifically, risk emerges from the reality that a given message will be received and understood in certain ways, and that this reception may not be the intended message of the source.

The following chapter discusses *audience* in more detail and also relates the concept known as the *imagined audience* as perhaps being most relevant to internet memes. It is the imagined audience which ultimately determines how the message will be understood, regardless of actual intent, or as Hall would call it, the preferred or dominant meaning of a text.

References

Berger, J. (2016). *Contagious: Why things catch on.* New York: Simon & Schuster.

Coldwell, W. (2015, May 22). Such precaution, very exits: Delta Airlines launches internet meme safety video. *The Guardian.* Retrieved from https://www.theguardian.com/travel/2015/may/22/delta-airlines-internet-meme-safety-video

Denny's Tumblr. (2016). *I'll have one coffee with meme and sugar.* [Tumblr blog]. Retrieved from http://blog.dennys.com/post/124541422335/hi-ill-have-one-coffee-with-meme-and-sugar

Dewey, C. (2015, September 8). How copyright is killing your favorite memes. *Washington Post.* Retrieved from https://www.washingtonpost.com/news/the-intersect/wp/2015/09/08/how-copyright-is-killing-your-favorite-memes/?noredirect=on&utm_term=.84d75ecbea6c

Eco, U. (1984). *Semiotics and the philosophy of language.* Hong Kong: Macmillan.

Frommer, D. (2009, March 24). Numa numa guy back in Geico commercial. *Business Insider.* Retrieved from http://www.businessinsider.com/numa-numa-guy-back-in-a-geico-commercial-2009-3?IR=T

Gee, J. P. (2004). *What video games have to teach us about learning and literacy.* New York: Palgrave MacMillan.

Giddens, A. (1984). *The constitution of society: Outline of the theory of structure.* Berkeley: University of California Press.

Ho, C. H. (2002). Hoffman v. Capital Cities/ABC, Inc. *Berkeley Technology Law Journal, 17*(1), 527–547.

Jenkins, H., Ford, S., & Green, J. (2013). *Spreadable media.* New York: New York University Press.

Knowyourmeme.com. (2010). *Success kid/I hate sandcastles.* Retrieved from http://knowyourmeme.com/memes/success-kid-i-hate-sandcastles

Knowyourmeme.com. (2013) *Numa Numa.* Retrieved from http://knowyourmeme.com/memes/numa-numa

McCrae, J. (2017, May 8). Meme marketing: How brands are speaking a new consumer language. *Forbes.* Retrieved from https://www.forbes.com/sites/forbescommunicationscouncil/2017/05/08/meme-marketing-how-brands-are-speaking-a-new-consumer-language/#3a5fe08c37f5

Morlin, B. (2016, September 28). Pepe joins (((echoes))) as new hate symbols. *Southern Poverty Law Center: Hate Watch.* Retrieved from https://www.splcenter.org/hatewatch/2016/09/28/pepe-joins-echoes-new-hate-symbols

Museum of Play (2018). *Where's the beef? The fast-food race game.* Retrieved from http://www.museumofplay.org/online-collections/3/48/112.2941

Nahon, K., & Hemsley, J. (2013). *Going viral.* Cambridge: Polity Press.

Nemetz, D. (2014, January 9). The inside story of the Wendy's 'where's the beef?' ad, 30 years later. *Yahoo Entertainment.* Retrieved from https://www.yahoo.com/entertainment/blogs/tv-news/inside-story-wendy-where-beef-ad-30-years-004259251.html?guccounter=1

Patel, R. (2013). First world problems: A fair use analysis of internet memes. *UCLA Entertainment Law Review, 20*(2), 235–256. Retrieved from https://papers.ssrn.com/sol3/papers.cfm?abstract_id=2426875

Pflaeging, J. (2015) Things that matter, pass them on: ListSite as viral online genre. 10Plus1: *Living Linguistics, 1,* 156–181. Retrieved from http://10plus1journal.com/wp-content/uploads/2015/09/12_JOU_ART_Pflaeging.pdf

Pountain, D., & Robins, D. (2000). *Cool rules: Anatomy of an attitude.* London: Reaktion.

Rath, J. (2017, March 2). Denny's is behind one of the most popular versions of the new 'zoom' meme. *Business Insider: Deutschland.* Retrieved from https://www.businessinsider.de/dennys-zoom-meme-2017-3?r=US&IR=T

Rocha, E. (2017). Y u no let me share memes?! – How meme culture needs a definitive test for noncommercial speech. *Journal of Art, Technology, & Property Law, 28*(37), 37–55.

Wiggins, B. E. (2016). Crimea river: Directionality in memes from the Russia-Ukraine conflict. *International Journal of Communication, 10,* 451–495.

6   Audience

Considering memes in general, with no specification for politics, culture, entertainment, or as a simple mechanism for humor, it is tempting to wonder about *audience* – in terms of who the audience is, how it is addressed, etc. Yet, *audience* is a loaded term, and it should not be applied to memes as one would apply the term to the audience of a film or advertisement. For internet memes, *audience* implies that their construction is to appeal to the desires or proclivities of particular groups of people who demonstrate certain characteristics or share certain commonalities, whether demographic, psychographic, or algorithmic. The traditional treatment of *audience* does not fit well with internet memes because such an approach assumes a top-down mode of expression. In the course of this chapter, I suggest that several factors must be considered instead of presuming the existence of an *audience* with regard to memes. Agency, polysemy, and the role of the media narrative represent crucial factors to analyze before considering a meme's audience. To support this view, it is first helpful to understand how *audience* has been understood in media research.

Audiences and the Reception of Content, Historically

Before going into more detail with respect to internet memes and *audience,* it is important to explore how the term has been understood and applied historically. Those earlier questions sought to learn more about whether and to what degree certain messages may have an *effect* on an *audience* or what drives an individual to use and seek out certain messages. Similar questions also relate to internet memes, as will be revealed in the course of this chapter.

Three primary assumptions define how audience has been understood over decades of media research, and these are addressed in what follows. First, to posit the existence of an audience, regardless of the content consumed, is to suggest that the individuals who comprise it share certain characteristics, such as an affinity for the content or the capacity to understand it. This is an important point with respect to internet memes as much research on the subject has tended to favor English-language memes. Thus, for a meme in Paraguay or Austria, for example, if one speaks of an audience, it is likely to be a localized audience, especially in terms of current issues relevant to that area. In my analysis of the memes that emerged from the Russian annexation of Crimea in 2014, and with respect to *audience* as a concept, I introduced the term *directionality* to correspond to a polarizing effect, which assumes a dichotomous relationship. That relationship, however, is tethered to local contexts. Even the manner of issuing an insult to Russians or Ukrainians required a close reading of each cultural context (Wiggins, 2016).

Second, an audience typically *receives* the content and is not usually able or inclined to respond. This is a historical assumption based on approaches to old media: namely that radio, newspapers, television, etc. as forms of mass communication address a mass audience. With internet memes, responses are generally *desired* by those who post or curate; however, a distinction should be made in regard to what is understood as *response*. A meme posted on Instagram, 4chan or a subreddit is likely also to function as a way to get responses from those who agree with the meme's content. Alternatively, a meme posted to elicit judgmental and negative responses is viewed as trolling or shitposting. The point is that a *response* is relative depending on the ideological practice at work and also evinces memes as artifacts of digital culture in the sense of their capacity to encourage *purposeful* production and consumption.

Third, an audience may be affected by the content it consumes, but perhaps more importantly, the reason for use and the potential for satisfaction gained from use is important to consider when discussing *audience* and any form of mediated content. This perspective requires further deliberation in the following section.

Beyond Effects: Uses and Gratifications

Much of the research that led to explorations of media use and its audiences emerged from the postpositivist studies, which investigated the potential effects of media, such as fears associated with the power of propaganda in the Payne Fund studies (Lowery & DeFleur, 1995). Such studies positioned *audience* as a passive mass ready to receive content, thus stoking fears of propaganda and control. Critics of this perspective, such as John Dewey (1927), proposed that through education people could be strengthened intellectually and that, in general, people were capable of choosing and using media wisely. The move from examining media effects to the reasons why audiences use media and what they get in return for their use emerged in the work of Paul Lazarsfeld and, later, with Herta Herzog. In fact, it was Herzog's (1944) article on the "motivations and gratifications" of radio soap opera audiences that led to a more audience-centric view of media research.

Herzog's work led to the *uses and gratifications* approach to media research (Baran & Davis, 2009). This approach was less interested in media effects and looked more at the choices people make in media consumption. Specifically, this approach asked "why do people intentionally buy a particular kind of magazine or book, turn first to a particular section of the newspaper, or scan the radio and TV schedules to locate certain programs?" (Lowery & DeFleuer, 1995, p. 400). Similarly, Wilbur Schramm, who is responsible for instituting "communications" as an academic discipline and developed one of the first models of communication, offered the *fraction of selection* to ascertain why people select certain forms of mass communication. Schramm's *fraction of selection* positions the expectation of reward divided by the effort required to indicate the frequency of taking part in the activity. Basically, the least amount of effort required will likely lead to the greatest or most satisfying reward. For example, if you wanted to determine why a person reads a lot or very little, you could apply the *fraction of selection*. First you need to determine the rewards and then the effort required, or the difficulties associated with the activity. For rewards, this could be social status, career advancement, information, taking a break, etc. For difficulties, not having the time, resources, or supportive social peers could encourage a person not to engage in reading. If the difficulties are severe enough, the rewards may not matter, and a decline in reading will occur. Applied to internet memes, you could ask why people share memes about an issue of social importance (political, cultural, economic, etc.) as opposed to taking real-world action regarding the same issue. The answer likely lies in the question of the required effort. Arguably, more effort is required for a person to take part in a social movement than to share memes. Yet, it is the tantalizing aspect of virality and networked participation structures which likely suggest why it is easier and more enjoyable to take part in meme creation and curation than in social movements or related activities.

To summarize, *audience* signifies certain specific assumptions in earlier media research but also with regard to its application to internet memes. These assumptions pertain to audience characteristics; the reception of and possibility of a response to a given message; and, the uses and gratifications ascribed or gained by a given individual or audience. Finally, I offer an estimation of Schramm's *function of selection* for internet memes as discursive units in digital culture. However, one limitation to my contribution lies in the fact that memes are necessarily polysemic. With multiple meanings and interpretations seemingly possible, a tighter focus is needed. The next section emphasizes perspectives from Stuart Hall with respect to the manner by which interpretation occurs by an individual or audience.

Stuart Hall: Dominant, Negotiated, and Oppositional Decoding

Like internet memes specifically, Hall asserts that most media or texts are polysemic. For a text to have multiple meanings suggests that interpretation figures prominently, thus elevating the freedom or liberating aspect of meaning as situated within the individual, poised to unpack one or more of several possible meanings. Hall claims that it is the producer of a message who constructs a preferred or dominant reading of the message. With a preferred reading, a producer of a given message speaks to those individuals presumed to hold a similar view in the message sent. Should there be disagreement or perhaps misunderstanding with the intended or preferred (dominant) reading of a given message, Hall says that a *negotiated* meaning emerges. Hall (2012) states that "[n]egotiated codes operate through what we might call particular or situated logics: and these logics are sustained by their differential and unequal relation to the discourses and logics of power" (p. 143). Essentially, a negotiated reading occurs when an individual perceives and possibly accepts the preferred reading but also incorporates one's own social position, background, experiences, values, etc. in the process of decoding the message. A negotiated reading may result in a binary understanding of a given text; a person sees and understands the message in terms of its preferred (dominant) reading but also additionally holds a reading which may involve contradictions, disagreement, etc. A further type of reading Hall introduces is *oppositional*. This occurs when an individual receives the message, understands the preferred reading, but decodes the message in a way that is in direct opposition to the dominant reading.

As an example, a photograph from the 2018 G-7 summit in Charlevoix, Canada, was remixed critically into a meme, but in fact both versions, the original (included as Figure 6.1) and remix, offer opportunities to understand Hall's decoding methods and also illuminate the question of *audience* with respect to digital discursive practices.

The preferred reading of the initial image is already problematic. Interpreting it to mean that Trump is weak or that his efforts are hurting

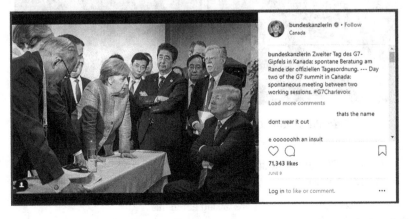

Figure 6.1 Chancellor Angela Merkel's Iconic Instagram Photo of the G-7 Summit.

the USA and its allies is likely only possible given a person's ideological practice aligned with such interpretation and, perhaps more importantly, this depends highly on where it is deployed (online or off) and what language is used to address it. Naturally, the pragmatics of context must also be considered when analyzing memes, given a desire to understand the intended *audience*.

The original image was uploaded by German Chancellor Angela Merkel's team to her official Instagram account with the rather unremarkable text "spontaneous meeting between two working groups" (Merkel, 2018). If the preferred reading is anything, it at least acknowledges that the 2018 G-7 summit was qualitatively different for no other reason than Trump's unconventional rhetorical approach to staunch allies of the USA. Beyond that negotiated readings abound: Merkel is in a dominant position, and Trump recoils; Trump is dominant and center, others look to him for guidance, etc. Interestingly, and as an example of a negotiated reading from a non-G-7 country, the official newspaper of the Chinese Communist Party tweeted "two meetings on the same day" to show the degree of contrast between the G-7 and the Xi-Putin meeting as part of the Shanghai Cooperation Organization summit. The tweeted photo highlights the perceived lack of harmony in the G-7 by showing Xi and Putin walking in unison and appearing authoritative and in control, shown in Figure 6.2.

Figure 6.2 People's China Daily Tweet.

Here, the perspectives offered by Hall grant a method to read internet memes in such a way to realize multiple interpretations simultaneously. However, such a feat is likely only accomplished with a critical capacity for analysis and an acknowledgement of the semiotic process at work in memes that build meaning *and makes things seem to mean something.* The catch here is agency: alongside political readings of memes and despites affordances from Hall, individuals are nevertheless routinely involved in meaning creation and curation. The degree to which a meme affects a person's worldview is largely dependent upon the *media narrative* incorporated in the meme. Before fully and contextually defining the term *media narrative,* a first brief case study will clarify how internet memes relate to *audience* as discussed thus far.

Toward a Meme-Centric Understanding of Audience

What is critical to consider is that audiences of audiovisual media, such as television and film, are constructed in the sense that a media organization produces content which addresses a given group of people according both to their presumed interests and to the intentions of the particular media organization. Applying the same reasoning to internet memes misses the role agency plays in online spaces. The *White Woman Calls the Cops* meme that surfaced in May 2018 serves as an example for this discussion of *audience.*

The meme emerges from a YouTube video which depicts an unidentified white woman wearing sunglasses and holding a smart phone to her ear with what appears to be an emotionless expression. The meme follows the insertion-in-older-images subgenre in which a person's image is inserted into another context, often with some historical significance. The *White Woman Calls the Cops* meme, also known as the #BBQ-Becky meme, remixed the woman as calling the cops during the historic speech given by Dr Martin Luther King, Jr or sitting on the same bus as Rosa Parks, as depicted in Figure 6.3. For a bit of background, the unknown woman was calling the police to report a small group of African Americans who were using a charcoal grill in a public park in Oakland, California. Apparently, the specific spot chosen by the grillers was not in a charcoal-designated area.

This is a similar case compared to a former employee of a Philadelphia-based Starbucks who called the police to report a few African American men waiting inside the café as they were expecting friends. As ironically noted by a journalist writing for the online magazine *The Root,* which focuses on black popular culture and news, "two men were arrested in a Center City Starbucks café for possession of blackness with intent to exist" (Harriot, 2018). The difference in that case was that the police actually arrested the two African American men simply for being inside the Starbucks. Figure 6.4 shows another iteration of the

Figure 6.3 White Woman Calls Cops, Rosa Parks.

Figure 6.4 The Root's Instagram Photo of *White Woman Calls Cops* aka #BBQBecky.

White Woman Calls Cops meme, uploaded to *The Root*'s Instagram account on May 14, 2018.

The obvious contextual implication (or following Hall, the preferred or dominant reading) should be clear: the unknown woman's actions indicate racial tensions exacerbated by overreactions in the USA, especially with regard to increased incidents of police violence (such as black males aged 15–34 being approximately nine times more likely to be killed in 2016 [Swaine & McCarthy, 2017]).

With regard to *audience*, it seems incorrect to assume that these memes were created to address an audience, at least when compared to a more general understanding of *audience*. It is more helpful and sensible not to think of a meme's *audience* but rather to view the *White Woman Calls Cops* meme as a discursive unit of digital culture: its point is to address the issue of racial tensions in the USA and also white privilege. Do these issues have specific *audiences*? Or is it perhaps more helpful to think of these and similarly socio-cultural, political issues as concerning communities or even *publics*?

Grunig and Hunt's (1984) treatment of a situational theory of publics may be helpful to clarify why when thinking about internet memes, particularly those which offer some form of social or cultural critique as with the *White Woman Calls Cops* meme, *audience* as a concept may be misleading. Basically, a public is aware of an issue and may want to do something about the issue. For example, anyone who is concerned about climate change/global warming is at a minimum part of a public, which shares the same concerns, even though the individuals themselves may not be aware of each other. Similarly, Grunig and Hunt (1984) argue further that individuals must be able to recognize a problem and to assess the level of desired involvement in a given issue. Furthermore, and perhaps most elucidating with regard to internet memes and their role in digital culture, individuals are either inclined to seek information actively or to process information as it comes to them.

Viewing such socio-critical, cultural examples is helpful as it demonstrates that while digital culture effectively produces content rather rapidly, the propensity for taking real-world action appears less salient. Again, in reference to Grunig and Hunt (1984), in general, people must recognize both the problem and the degree to which a person may be constrained by internal/external forces to become involved in order for action even to be a consideration. Grunig (1997) notes that if the issues occur in the real world, external to the person, then "changes must be made in a person's environment before his or her perceptions ... and communication behavior will change" (p. 25). Perhaps, internet memes can be the means by which the public gain access to more information thus encouraging social engagement. Interestingly, Marichal (2013) introduces the term *microactivism* to signify forms of daily engagement in posts, comments, reactions, etc. and suggests that the political purpose is maintained even though mass mobilization does not take place. Marichal cites examples such as dedicated Facebook pages, Twitter accounts, sharing and reacting to posts online as indicative of *microactivism*. Further, Petray's (2013, in Frazer & Carlson, 2017) notion of *self-writing*, pertaining specifically to the experience of Indigenous peoples, offers an opportunity for *microactivism* on a daily basis through posts, comments, etc. Similarly, Lenhardt (2016) discusses the ways in which internet memes are used in American Indian activism as being a kind of "low-cost activism", which assists in the effort to feel part of a larger group, emphasize cohesiveness and a sense of belonging among disparately located individuals (p. 80). Leveraging internet memes on social media for purposes of perceived activism can be purposeful, but the impact of the purpose (positive or negative, etc.) is relative to the group's ideological practice.

Before moving into the description of *media narrative* as it relates to *audience* and why this applies to internet memes, I present a brief overview of the ways audience is understood in relationship to televised content, whether entertainment or news. The role of the news media is largely to reproduce utterances, stances, perspectives, etc. which derive from the dominant, hegemonic system. Ideally, news media report on issues and events that are seemingly important to individuals who form part of a civil society. Additionally, entertainment serves a discursive function for the expression of social and cultural values. However, both news and entertainment media transmit information that help constitute popular culture. For Hall (1981), *popular* culture "is the ground on which the transformations are worked" (p. 228). However, that ground is constructed based on an unequal power balance favoring media elites. This power may be limited such as when a news media organization has concerns about losing an advertiser due to perceived controversial content or the need to focus on an issue or present a politically charged issue in such a way to avoid alienating larger segments of the *audience*. It is still up to individuals to make sense of the mediated content they so enjoyably consume. The advantages attributed to elite producers of media content signify how a capitalist system reifies its own self-preservation by constantly producing media *texts* which are by and large *soft copies*, that is, remixes and/or reproductions of known and familiar genres (Berkun, 2010; Lenthem, 2007). In entertainment, this often takes the form of reboots of older series or a reimagining of already established genres. In news media, this process occurs iteratively in the form of an endless 24/7 news cycle, incessant breaking news stories, and the digital entanglement of news-as-social media. Furthermore, an additional feature of news media is the propensity to emphasize certain points or perspectives over others, distribute concerns, frame the issue in such a way and for such a purpose, etc.

The catch here is that on the one hand Hall suggests that individuals can still make up their own minds about mediated content, and that different interpretations are possible. On the other hand, however, is the contention that entertainment and news media operate in a way that ensures their continued survival in the capitalist system. Taken together, the implication is that televised content, especially the news, can have real-world effects depending on how the *media narrative* is constructed and communicated. This is an important point as internet memes which critique a real-world person or event are necessarily also drawing on a media narrative (Wiggins, 2017).

With respect to *audience*, individuals who interact with one another (be it one-to-many, many-to-one, many-to-many, etc.) do so with certain assumptions about the real-world. Indeed, these assumptions may be individual fabrications, delusions, etc. or they may be the end result of how certain knowledge and ideas are transmitted through *media narratives*.

Consisting of three basic points, a media narrative is malleable depending upon the ability to ask critical questions; it has the capacity to shape opinion as well as perceptions of reality and a person's decision-making process; and, perhaps most importantly it incorporates linguistic and image-based simulations of real-world events, which adhere and/or appeal to ontologically specific perspectives, which may include the un/intentional use of stereotyping, ideology, allegory, etc.

Media Narratives, Television, and Internet Memes

A *media narrative* operates as a vehicle for conveying information in the form of news or related story-types (Wiggins, 2017). Within internet memes, the function and impact of the *media narrative* has the propensity to distort reality. This is due to referencing real-world events contextualized by a particular media narrative. The largely unavoidable inclusion of a media narrative in internet memes means that reality may be depicted in a way that is in line with an individual's or group's ideological practice, regardless of whether it has any relevance on real, objective truth. Media narratives permeate news stories in all media but perhaps most prodigiously in the four screen-types, or TV, laptop and/or PC, smartphone, and tablet. Choosing to get news from television or online, including social media, may be a question of age (Nielsen & Sambrook, 2016), but regardless of the actual screen-type media narratives abound.

A media narrative is constructed semiotically through the use of connotative meanings. For example, after a tragic event such as a natural disaster, a school shooting, or a crisis brought about by civil war, news media invariably construct a narrative around the event. Certain key words, points of emphasis, images, possibly even music or sound effects, etc. can be deployed purposefully to impact the reception of the message.

A central accompaniment with media narratives is *opposition*, especially if the topic is controversial or polarizing. For example, if two heads of state meet, a news story reporting this will likely include an image of the two individuals shaking hands or sitting near one another or possibly a combination of these possibilities. If the meeting occurs during a period of tension, opposition exists in the form of how *stability* is negotiated with an (imagined) audience. Thus, the main function of such a report is to assuage concerns about a debilitating situation. Phrases such as "engaged in open conversation", "mutually beneficial", and/or "productive talks", etc. verbally communicate what is represented in an accompanying image. Rhetorical devices are deployed to ameliorate perceived tension among agents, states, groups, etc. but this tension may also be a further intentional construction built into the media narrative. The two potential poles of opposition (here in this example *instability* and *stability*) clearly elevate one (stability) for a specific purpose consonant with the function of a given media narrative. The pole likely does not change in emphasis.

Within internet memes, however, the relationship between two oppositional poles can be molded at whim. In fact, one of the functions of the internet meme is to upend or at least challenge a dominant narrative. The media narrative adds to the intertextual nature of internet memes, but it is worthwhile to consider the ways in which this and other postmodern features are shared between memes and television.

Postmodern Tendencies of Television and Internet Memes

While memes tend to rely heavily on intertextuality, television both intentionally and incidentally employs intertextuality in various genres and across all of the four screen types. As a term *audience* should be malleable to allow for the affordances, limitations, or inherent differences between and among these types. It may be best to view the postmodern turn in television as a precursor to the highly versatile nature of internet memes. The reliance on intertextuality is but one of many aspects shared by content across the four-screen types and internet memes.

Television underwent a centralizing development toward incorporating postmodern tendencies in the content it broadcast from approximately the late 1980s onward. Specifically, Lash (1990) contends that a movement toward postmodern television is marked especially by "aesthetic self-consciousness/self-reflexiveness; juxtaposition/montage/ bricolage; paradox/ambiguity/uncertainty; intertextuality and the blurring of genre boundaries; irony, parody and pastiche" (in Barker, 2012, p. 355). While Lash's perspective that television developed postmodern tendencies, the same applies to internet memes, in terms of semiotic and intertextual construction. This corresponds primarily to those memes which have a critical discursive function.

As examples consider one or more of the following internet memes from 2016 onward as belonging to one or more of the aforementioned postmodern markers: *Distracted Boyfriend, He Protec but He also Attac, Trump Orb, Mocking SpongeBob, Meryl Streep Singing, The Babadook* (discussed in Chapter 7), *American Chopper, The Return of Palpatine, Salt Bae*, and many more. The *American Chopper* multi-panel meme of screenshots from the reality TV series, which ceased production in 2010, gained widespread social media presence in 2017 and 2018 (Yglesias, 2018). Its function combines intertextuality, self-reflexiveness, juxtaposition, irony and pastiche, and accomplishes this through a series of visual arguments in the form of a proposition, rebuttal, reaffirmation, second rebuttal, and a final statement.

Similarly, *The Return of Palpatine* features screenshots of the character from the *Star Wars* film *The Revenge of the Sith*. In one image-macro two-panel meme, a scene is juxtaposed with Palpatine's response "I am the Senate". In the top image from a parody skit called *Hell's Cafeteria*, chef Gordan Ramsay holds a slice of bread on either side of a woman's head and asks the woman what she is, to which she replies that she is an idiot sandwich. Internet memes are perfect vehicles for the merging and mashing of Lash's (1990) postmodern markers. These examples express more about an *intertextual reference* than a particular *audience*. Once again, I must emphasize the communicative function of internet memes. In some cases, the point is purely ludic; in other cases, the purpose of the meme is to offer critique; still in many cases, the purpose is a combination of ludic and critical. The postmodern markers discussed above and the media narrative work in tandem in the construction of internet memes. Together they form the essence of a semiotic toolkit for meaning making within memes.

The subsequent section applies the concept of the *imagined* audience to internet memes. Its chief purpose is to link intent with creation, without however, any need to question an internet meme's "author" (indeed, this perspective is extended further in Chapter 7 with respect to contributions from Michel Foucault). However, the postmodern markers are stylistic choices in the construction of meaning within memes, where the media narrative represents something potentially insidious. The media narrative can seem real and factual despite being perhaps partially true or blatantly biased, objectively seen. How an event is conveyed in a media narrative and how this translates into how individuals perceive reality all pertain to the fragility of truth peddled in the form of critically formulated memes.

Internet Memes and the *Imagined* Audience

While the previous sections have discussed whether it makes sense to talk of *audiences* with regard to memes, the relationship among media narratives, television, and internet memes, it is helpful to examine a few instances in which certain internet memes do, in fact, have an audience.

Specifically, audiences exist in particular and contextualized examples. Memes have audiences on YouTube (Shifman, 2012; Xu, Park, Kim, & Park, 2016), when an issue polarizes individuals (Wiggins, 2016), or more generally as Milner (2012, p. 167) notes that memes inhere "discursive truths for a situated audience". However, the term *audience* with regard to internet memes requires some adjustment.

The term *imagined audience* better captures the kinds of mental processes involved in thinking of audiences and memes. Several researchers, such as Marwick and boyd (2010), Baym and boyd (2012), and Litt (2012) discuss the concept of the audience as an *imagined* construction. They suggest that an *imagined audience* is one addressed through interaction with various forms of social media. As an example, if a person creates a message on Instagram or Facebook, that person has in mind a particular group, types of people, or perhaps a number of specific (and real) people. However, these same hypothetical or real people may or may not even receive the message or its intended (encoded) meaning.

If a person posts an internet meme to Instagram, that person's motivation for doing so has something to do with the people the person has in mind at the time of posting. This motivation is largely informed by the assumption of certain characteristics consonant with both the thematic aspects of the internet meme and with the imagined audience. This is a process indelibly connected to the construction and negotiation of *identity*, which is discussed in greater detail in the following chapter. To close this chapter and this particular section on the *imagined audience,* I wish to refer to a concept I introduced in a study of memes that emerged from the Crimean crisis in 2014 between Russia and Ukraine. As a concept, *directionality* simultaneously discloses at least two audiences, namely (1) the audience poised to appreciate the critique (often engineered as humor) and (2) the audience targeted with the criticism. In both instances, while more is known about whom the meme addresses, the utility of the conceptual gains offered by *imagined audience* remains. The disclosing audiences demonstrate awareness of what a particular meme signifies directionally. As such *directionality* reveals the boundaries of a group regarding a given issue; *imagined audience* suggests that the process of expressing ourselves ultimately still means that certain assumptions exist about who we are in relationship to memes as a cultural commodity and to each other. These assumptions are guided performatively by the construction and negotiation of identity. Appropriately, the following chapter investigates *identity* and internet memes.

References

Baran, S. J., & Davis, D. K. (2009). *Mass communication theory: Foundations, ferment, future.* (5th ed.). Boston, MA: Wadsworth Cengage.

Barker, C. (2012). *Cultural studies: Theory and practice* (4th ed.). London: Sage.

Baym, N. K., & boyd, d. (2012). Socially mediated publicness: An introduction. *Journal of Broadcasting & Electronic Media, 56*(3), 2012, 320–329.

Berkun, S. (2010). *The myths of innovation*. Sebastopol, CA: O'Reilly.

Dewey, J. (1927). *The public and its problems*. New York: Holt.

Frazer, R., & Carlson, B. (2017). Indigenous memes and the invention of a people. *Social Media + Society*, October–December. 1–12.

Grunig, J. E. (1997). A situational theory of publics: Conceptual history, recent challenges and new research. In D. Moss, T. MacManus, & D. Vercic (Eds.), *Public relations research: An international perspective.* (pp. 3–48). London: International Thomson Business Press.

Grunig, J. E., & Hunt, T. (1984). *Managing public relations*. New York: Holt, Rinehart and Winston.

Hall, S. (1981). Notes on deconstructing 'The Popular'. In R. Samuel (Ed.), *People's History and Socialist Theory:* (pp. 227–240). London: Routledge.

Hall, S. (2012). Encoding/decoding. In M. G. Durham & D. M. Kellner (Eds.), *Media and cultural studies: Keyworks.* (pp. 137–144). Malden, MA: Wiley-Blackwell.

Harriot, M. (2018, June 8). Philadelphia police department changes trespassing policy after Starbucks incident. *The Root*. Retrieved from: https://www.theroot.com/philadelphia-cops-change-trespassing-policy-after-starb-1826683547

Herzog, H. (1944). Motivations and gratifications of daily serial listeners. In P. F. Lazarsfeld & F. N. Stanton (Eds.), *Radio research, 1942–1943*. New York: Duell, Sloan and Pearce.

Lash, S. (1990). *Sociology of postmodernism*. London and New York: Routledge.

Lenhardt, C. (2016). "Free Peltier now!" The use of internet memes in American Indian activism. *American Indian Culture and Research Journal 40*(3), 67–84.

Lenthem, J. (2007, February). The ecstasy of influence: A plagiarism. *Harper's Magazine*. Retrieved from: https://harpers.org/archive/2007/02/the-ecstasy-of-influence/

Litt, E. (2012). *Knock, knock.* Who's there? The imagined audience. *Journal of Broadcasting & Electronic Media, 56*(3), 330–345.

Lowery, S. A., & DeFleur, M. L. (1995). *Milestones in mass communication research.* (3rd ed.). White Plains, NY: Longman.

Marichal, J. (2013). Political Facebook groups: Micro-activism and the digital front stage. *First Monday, 18*, Article 12.

Marwick, A. E., & boyd, d. (2010). I tweet honestly, I tweet passionately: Twitter users, context collapse, and the imagined audience. *New Media & Society, 13*(1), 114–133. doi:10.1177/1461444810365313.

Merkel, Bundeskanzlerin. (2018, June 9). [*Photo of the G7 Summit*]. Retrieved from: https://www.instagram.com/p/Bjz0RKtAMFp/

Milner, R. M. (2012). *The world made meme: Discourse and identity in participatory media.* (PhD thesis). The University of Kansas, Lawrence, KS.

Nielsen, R. K., & Sambrook, R. (2016). What is happening to television news? *Digital News Project 2016.* Reuters Institute for the Study of Journalism. Retrieved from https://reutersinstitute.politics.ox.ac.uk/sites/default/files/2017-06/What%20is%20Happening%20to%20Television%20News.pdf

Shifman, L. (2012). An anatomy of a YouTube meme. *New Media & Society, 14*(2), 187–203.

Swaine, J., & McCarthy, C. (2017, January 8). Young black men again faced highest rate of US police killings in 2016. *The Guardian: The Counted*. Retrieved from: https://www.theguardian.com/us-news/2017/jan/08/the-counted-police-killings-2016-young-black-men

Wiggins, B. E. (2016). Crimea river: Directionality in memes from the Russia-Ukraine conflict. *International Journal of Communication, 10*(2016), 451–495.

Wiggins, B. E. (2017). Navigating an immersive narratology: Fake news and the 2016 U.S. Presidential campaign. *International Journal of E-Politics, 8*(3), 16–33. doi:10.4018/IJEP.2017070101

Yglesias, M. (2018, April 10). The *American Chopper* meme, explained. *Vox*. Retrieved from: https://www.vox.com/2018/4/10/17207588/american-chopper-meme

Xu, W. W., Park, J. Y., Kim, J. Y., & Park, H. W. (2016). Networked cultural diffusion and creation on YouTube: An analysis of YouTube memes. *Journal of Broadcasting & Electronic Media, 60*(1), 104–122.

7 Identity

Investigating internet memes means acknowledging human nature especially with regard to the ways in which individuals view themselves and present themselves to each other, both online and off. Accordingly, identity is integral in an investigation of internet memes. Prior to a series of case studies that specifically address and demonstrate the ways in which memes are deployed as a part of a deterministic identity construction, it is essential to review previous scholarship on identity.

Identity as a concept has a wide range of definitive stances, from the philosophical to the political, from the cultural to the postmodern. Intrinsically, it remains a concept of import when it is desirable to understand the manner by which identity is constructed. My perspective of identity with respect to internet memes is largely based on Judith Butler's work on gender; in addition my view of identity also benefits from perspectives introduced by Anthony Giddens, to be discussed in a later section. Butler (1988) writes that "gender is in no way a stable identity or locus of agency from which various acts proceed; rather, it is an identity tenuously constituted in time – an identity instituted through a *stylized repetition of acts*" (p. 519, italics in original). Its fluid state of being depends on the recursive "stylized repetition of acts" and is an excellent way to understand how identity is constructed, similar to how discourse creates certain items of knowledge. It is the communicative exchange of textual, verbal, visual, etc. cues that negotiate identity. However, one's ideological practice invariably acts to constrain and/or liberate what is possible for one's identity.

Essentialism and Constructivism

Two major approaches to identity seek a universal understanding of identity, namely essentialism and constructivism. The former presupposes that a person inheres a certain essence that makes them that way and not another way, while the latter asserts that a person's identity is socially constructed. Laclau (1977) echoes the social constructivist view by arguing that discursive concepts, such as identity, are temporarily constructed and are at least partially established by hegemonic forces.

The emphasis on hegemony as the source of identity construction from a social constructivist view reminds of the process of ideological interpellation of the individual into a subject; this discussion of identity follows a similar trajectory.

The social constructivist approach has more relevance to internet memes because of the degree to which language, expression, and meaning intersect in constructivist, poststructuralist, and even postmodern approaches to identity. The semiotic construction of internet memes translates into the inclusion of multiple references to popular culture as well as combinations of image, video, text, etc. to negotiate meaning.

Furthermore, it is useful to explore the literature on identity construction relevant to the later discussion of identity and internet memes, specifically those perspectives which situate an argument based on critical-cultural theory.

Temporality and Instability of Identity

Identity is always something that is temporary and relatively unstable, and it is largely constructed through marking difference. An in-group's identity exists because of the *acknowledgement of what it is because of what it is not*, that is, it lacks the qualities of the out-group's identity because it is different. The temporality and instability of identity inhere some degree of anxiety in the acknowledgement that one's self, one's assumed identity is not stable, but in flux. The anxiety fuels the motivation to recursively maintain identity through performative acts consonant with the proclivities of a given identity. Additionally, identity involves polarized dichotomies such as man/woman in which one category /man/ necessitates *other*, an opposite category, which could be viewed as deviant, subservient, or simply inferior to the *initial* category. Judith Butler (2004) notes how individuals, upon learning about the birth of a child, almost immediately

> ...ask about certain sexually differentiated anatomical traits because we assume that those traits will in some sense determine that child's social destiny, and that destiny, whatever else it is, is structured by a gender system predicated upon the alleged naturalness of binary oppositions and, consequently, heterosexuality.
>
> (p. 31)

Heterosexuality becomes a precondition, an expectation for human identity in normative terms, and any sexuality that is different is exactly that, understood as oppositional to the assumed precondition and therefore deviant, subordinate, etc. In her discussion of the attributes *man* and *woman* with respect to *gender*, Butler's main argument is partially to reconsider conceptualizations of gender in order to situate it less as a stable precondition but rather as changing, as performative. Indeed, Butler (1990, p. 25) posits that "gender proves to be performative – that is, constituting the identity it is purported to be. In this sense, gender is always a doing, though not a doing by a subject who might be said to preexist the deed". This notion of gender as performative underscores the degree to which ideological practice takes hold on the individual; similarly, *identity* is performative, it is interpellated, or addressed, by structural features of the social system one happens to inhabit. Adjustments or changes to gender or identity that fall outside of preconditional expectations are therefore deviant and worthy of marginalization. I say this not to advance a judgment but as a critical reading of identity.

Identity originates in language and is maintained through discourse – this is especially associated with Lacan and with respect to the expression or enactment of power per Foucault. This is present in terms of applications of abstract words such as *freedom, human rights, terrorism*, etc. One person's *terrorist* is another person's *freedom fighter*. This Foucauldian perspective further elaborates the point that *identity* is a category that is purposefully constructed within discursive practices in which – through the exercise of power – certain groups emerge or are created through the demarcation of difference and thus the same groups – again, created within discourse – are justifiably treated in specific ways (positive or negative).

Internet memes are emblematic of identity construction in online spaces. However, this is not necessarily a process saturated by positivity and well-intended actions. In many cases, the demarcation of identity is accomplished through apoplectic expressions directed at an assumed other. This process occurs, perhaps at least in part, to counteract the anxiety within identity maintenance. Such efforts seek to maintain some semblance of stability and permanence despite identity essentially being in flux.

It is in the work of Anthony Giddens (1991) where the effects of fragmentation on identity reveal themselves. His discussion is one that is rooted within the analysis of globalization and its effects on individuals and social life, but it is equally relevant to online spaces given the dynamics of human–computer interaction. Specifically, Giddens introduces the term *disembeddedness* and *disembedding*. Essentially, these terms suggest conceptually that individuals are disembedded, or lifted out of their *original* contexts due to the relativization afforded by information and communication technologies, and surely also the vast array of social media platforms, as a consequence of late capitalism.

For Giddens, identity is at once process and product, an undertaking that must be continuously adjusted and maintained. Further, the inevitable struggle to build an identity and therefore a sense of belonging to a group, community, etc. online or off, necessarily implies engagement with consumer culture and all it offers. In order to achieve social salience, individuals construct their identity also as a consequence of acquiring material possessions. A link emerges between Giddens' perspective on identity and the Althusserian view of ideology as an enabling yet also constraining force: in order to *participate* in a group, a person must express certain messages or inclinations that conform to the group's identity (also in terms of what it is not). With respect to online discursive practices of internet memes, Giddens' views on identity suggest that late modernity encourages individuals to seek out relationships that produce and reinforce forms of trust through persistent communication and the reflexive practices that such persistence implies. It is worthwhile to note that this applies to any group using digital technologies to mediate their communication. Tragedy can emerge when identity is in flux and efforts are made to elevate the inner group's importance over a perceived outer group or other, such as in the case with the use of Facebook in the Duterte regime in The Philippines to promote "a culture of vigilantism" or how community preferences helped Burmese carry out massacres of the Rohingya in Myanmar (Reed, 2018; Vaidhyanathan, 2018, p. 192). The point is that in the negotiation of identity, mediated forms of communication along with viral messages spread as memes, fake news, etc. all work together in the interest of the group's perceived ideological practice. The two case studies that follow explore how identity is negotiated in politically and socio-culturally different forms but with similar effectiveness.

As a first case study, this discussion investigates examples related to the LGBTQ+ community. The rationale for using LGBTQ+ examples is relatively simple: as noted by D. Travers Scott in his analysis of the *Leave Britney Alone* meme, "[e]vidence is not always majoritarian, particularly regarding subjugated peoples and stigmatized objects of knowledge" (2014, p. 309). The case study focuses on the so-called *Babadook* meme, and a second case involves the "March for Our Lives" movement that resulted in part from the school shooting that occurred on February 14, 2018 at Marjory Stoneman Douglas High School in Parkland, Florida, but also includes LGBTQ+ aspects.

The Babadook: Horror Movie Monster as a Gay Icon?

Internet memes sometimes come from unexpected places, but one consistent attribute is that memes help individuals and groups to share in a discourse. The internet is a conduit for discursive expression; identity construction occurs precipitously when individuals embrace, accept, or reject, etc. attributes that are consistent with a particular ideological practice. This can have positive or negative real-world effects. The *Babadook* meme offers a chance to perceive community-building, identity-reifying, progressive series of messages that at once address (or, interpellate) a group but also recursively reconstitute that group's identity. The following sections recount how the Babadook developed and what meaning it has had for the LGBTQ+ community.

Naturally my view does not presume a universal, homologous group identity as signifying LGBTQ+. Rather, and as with the literature on identity, any group or community's identity is in flux, changeable. Yet, in order for identity to be knowable and recognizable to the group, certain constitutive elements must be core to the identity but not necessarily universal, such as the pride flag. As an example, the pride flag is a symbol of anti-discrimination, gayness, same-sex love and attraction, etc. but it cannot be assumed to be shared or accepted by all who would identify as belonging (or not) to LGBTQ+. Similarly, I do not maintain that the Babadook became universally accepted or used in LGBTQ+. Rather, this case reveals how groups can deploy images to address some knowable, perceptible facet of their identity in order to maintain the identity and to show support.

The Babadook is a 2014 Australian supernatural psychological horror film in which the reading of an eponymous children's storybook results in the emergence of the Babadook character – a monster which feeds on fear and sows anxiety and paranoia. The character's accidental summoning and the subsequent attempts to '*get rid of it*' serve as metaphors for living life as a member of LGBTQ+. The sense of belonging to one's family, for example, is nuanced by marginalization if not also ostracization, given concerns about coming out to one's family and friends. Metaphorically, the push to put the Babadook back in the *closet* addresses the anxieties associated with '*being out*' as an LGBTQ+ individual. While the film was released in 2014, it was not until late 2016 and into 2017 that the Babadook developed as an image in the LGBTQ+ community. One particular meme features the actual film, *The Babadook*, as one of many options on *Netflix* in the category of LGBT movies, another depicts the monster from the film remixed as a gay pride icon beckoning the viewer to become *babashook*, shown in Figure 7.1.

An ensuing *Babadiscourse* (Hunt, 2017) occurred online including remixes of *RuPaul's Drag Race* to include a reference to the Babadook figure, a fake announcement that the Human Rights Campaign planned to honor the Babadook with a Visibility Award. Various other memetic remixes took place, such as the affixing of the Babadook visage to the pride flag as an online emblem of LGBTQ+ identity as well as real-world remixes such as T-shirts with the Babadook holding a pride flag or even people dressed up as the Babadook at LGBTQ+ pride parades.

Resonance: Babadook, Facebook, and Identity

One partial explanation for the presence of the Babadook on social media in 2016 and 2017 may be related to Facebook's *Celebrate Pride* page, which started on June 26, 2015, and the addition of an option to react

Figure 7.1 The Babadook, LGBTQ+ pride.

to a post with a pride flag button. Incidentally, the date of the Facebook page launch coincided with the Obergefell v. Hodges US Supreme Court ruling of the same date, which effectively legalized same-sex marriage. Facebook's own research department concluded that as a consequence of the ruling, the incidence of Facebook users *coming out* on the social media platform increased alongside demonstrations of support for the ruling and its implications for social and cultural relations (State & Wernerfelt, 2015).

Much of the dynamic participation and use of *The Babadook* in identity construction serendipitously occurred during June 2017, Pride Month for that year. As is common with many memes, there is a tendency for a surge in popularity and deployment of it followed by a period of awareness of the meme that usually either fades or is less seemingly pronounced as it was initially. Regardless of the ebb and flow of a meme's popularity, its use in identity construction with respect to the perspectives mentioned earlier deserves more analysis.

How does this case of *The Babadook* contribute to an understanding of identity construction in general but with specific reference to the LGBTQ+ community? Resonance is a concept that is useful in this discussion primarily because of the ways in which LGBTQ+ identity construction often inheres notions of support, solidarity, and compassion as well as anxiety, depression, and marginality. This point is echoed in Scott's (2014) work with the *Leave Britney Alone* meme in which he acknowledges that the individual responsible for the initial video, Chris Crocker, engages in "not merely a defense of a celebrity but a performance of a kind of male homosexuality" (p. 318). Further Scott notes that "Crocker interpellates viewers to become his protectors, simultaneously evoking empathy and vulnerability" (p. 318). Thus, *affective resonance* "refers to the positive feedback loops created by affect, and in particular to the tendency of someone witnessing the display of affect in another person to resonate with and experience the same affect in response" (Gibbs, 2013, p. 3, in Scott, 2014, p. 316). The deployment of the *Babadook* image as a meme is clearly an example of affective resonance, as is the tendency to show support in times of tragedy or during periods of commemoration of an individual or event, similar to the ways in which Facebook users deployed *Je suis Charlie* memes or changed their profile photos to show solidarity in the aftermath of a disaster or terrorist attack.

The difference with respect to the *Babadook* meme is what it represents about the community that adopted it. In my view, the Babadook functions as a *synecdoche*: a visual phrase used to represent a larger whole. In this case, it semiotically refers to the anxieties and pain that might be associated with coming out to one's family and friends (similar to the desire in the film to renounce and expel the Babadook). The adoption of the Babadook as a kind of temporary representative of LGBTQ+ also underscores the notion that identity is necessarily always also temporary and unstable – it needs to be recursively reified in order for members of the community to know with what they should identify, regardless of the community.

The Babadook meme exemplifies how the tools of social media offer individuals an opportunity to demonstrate and perceive some semblance of support, community, and therefore a reification of identity. Further, Jenkins, Ito, and boyd (2016) argue that the goal of a participatory culture – ostensibly one that includes all types of groups – is to "continually create contexts that are more participatory than before...participatory culture is not about creating a particular state of society, but about collectively engaging in an aspirational project that constantly challenges us to expand opportunities for meaningful participation" (p. 182). I applaud their implied optimism, and clearly the Babadook is a positive and supportive emblem for the LGBTQ+ community, at least during a certain point in time. However, Rubin and McClelland (2015) found that sexual orientation minorities in general but also those of color tend to express worry, anxiety, fear, etc. about unintentionally outing themselves and choose language online and posts carefully in order to conform with a hetereonormative discourse. Some scholars take a cyberintellectual position and extol social media for its emancipatory effect on a *participatory culture*. Others demonstrate that despite the liberating and/or socially progressive possibilities of social media, groups continue to exist comprised in part of individuals not yet ready to risk ostracization and marginalization. The Babadook as a meme (enthymeme, visual argument) functions as an excellent metaphor for this distinction.

It is in part my claim that the process of appropriating internet memes for the purpose of identity co-construction may ameliorate feelings of low self-esteem and anxiety, perhaps only temporarily, but functionally. As noted by Rubin and McClelland (2015, p. 514) in addition to identity construction in general but also with specific reference to sexual minorities that comprise LGBTQ+ communities, research into online environments has revealed them to be an important tool for enacting same-sex identities (Hillier & Harrison, 2007) and also serving as formative communities for supportive peer relationships (Fraser, 2010). Additionally, online environments such as social media aid in dealing with such issues as depression and self-harm (McDermott, Roen, & Piela, 2015). As discussed above, resonance, or more specifically affective resonance may also help explain the use of online tools in the construction of identity, especially for groups seeking empathy and support. Scott (2013) notes that resonance may also be understood as a form of intertextuality whereby the production, or in the case of memes the sharing and curation, and the consumption of media that address the aspects of a particular group's identity help to "amplify, clarify, and enrich sympathetic elements" (Scott, 2014, p. 316). What is implied here is a slightly altered version of intertextuality, but the sentiment is helpful. Applied to the Babadook meme and considering that sexual minorities indeed use online tools to assist in identity construction as well as community building, the intertextual resonance is achieved through the in-group's knowledge of the Babadook as indicative of the struggle to live life as LGBTQ+. Furthermore, this knowledge is then remixed visually in the form of memes to quickly encapsulate the sentiment for rapid consumption and reproduction, reifying the group's social structure and reconstituting identity.

The Babadook represents a type of meme that emerges due to interpretation which may not be the intention of the *author* of the source text, in this case the film. Given the rapidity by which memes are produced, curated, shared, remixed and iterated further, etc., the author indirectly expresses a silent abstention of participation: an individual creates a (likely remixed) meme that is part of an ongoing or already commenced discourse. Thus, the meme functions as an utterance, not to be cited to the person but to further, counter, or re-direct a discourse.

Viewing memes as texts, the identity of an author of a given meme is or at least should be unimportant. If we were to praise the authors of memes, we might begin to find ourselves biased toward a particular type or sub-genre of meme due simply to name recognition. The emergence of internet memes like the Babadook occurs spontaneously, whereas 4chan, reddit, Facebook, etc. often function as a kind of clearinghouse for the production and spread of internet memes. This point seeks not to devalue the function of memes produced in spaces designed specifically for their production and dissemination, but simply acknowledges that this difference exists and suggests further that memes can be and are used as a visual complement to human language, similar to emoticons and emojis. The subsequent section is a second case study and explores the role of internet memes in the aftermath of a tragic school shooting in the USA.

March for Our Lives: Aftermath of the Parkland School Shooting

On February 14, 2018, Nikolas Cruz booked an Uber driver to transport him to Marjory Stoneman Douglas high school. He remarked to the driver that he was going to his music class, possibly to distract attention from the backpack and duffel bag he was carrying in which he had placed an AR-15 assault rifle and approximately 150 rounds of ammunition (Neal, 2018). Upon entering the school, Cruz set off the fire alarm and began shooting people indiscriminately. It is worthwhile to point out that the AR-15 used was not only legally purchased but was acquired only after a successful background check had been conducted on Cruz. He killed 17 people ranging in ages from 14 to 49 and wounded 15 people.

On February 17, students and others held a Rally to Support Firearm Safety and Legislation in Florida. What emerged from this initial and rather raw and emotive reaction to the tragedy was a broad social movement culminating in the formation of a student-led gun control organization called *Never Again MSD* (Marjory Stoneman Douglas, the name of the high school). Hashtags #NeverAgain and #EnoughIsEnough permeated social media in the wake of the tragedy. A well-funded student-led demonstration occurred on March 24, 2018 in Washington D.C. and many other cities in the USA and globally with approximately 2 million participating in the USA of which about 800,000 marched in D.C. alone (Sit, 2018).

Internet responses to the student advocacy varied from support to vitriol, from leveraging social media for the purpose of building community to spreading fake news-oriented memes for the purpose of lampooning, if not also lambasting, the student activists. One particular series of internet memes features Emma Gonzalez, a student who survived the Parkland school shooting and gained international attention due to speeches given in the aftermath of the tragedy. In one example involving Gonzalez, the Facebook page managed for Representative Steve King, a Republican politician in Iowa, posted an image macro decrying Gonzalez's appearance and use of the Cuban flag on her jacket worn during her emotional speech given at the *March for Our Lives* demonstration on March 24, 2018. The meme gained over 6,000 reactions, of which over 3,000 were "likes" and over 2,000 were "angry faces", and, perhaps most importantly, was shared nearly 40,000 times, shown in Figure 7.2. In the nearly 7,000 comments, one can clearly see different discourses in action, with deep divisions obvious in a social media maelstrom of polarized and partially articulated views.

Several memes about Gonzalez spread online in the form of an animated GIF as well as an image-macro. In the meme, Gonzalez is shown tearing up a copy of the US Constitution. The GIF and image spread

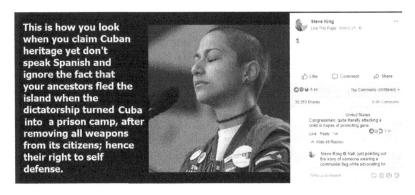

Figure 7.2 Remixing *March for Our Lives*.

virally online especially within groups with conservative, far-right, or alt-right political identities. The GIF was actually created by self-described right-leaning "free speech social network" called *Gab* and was tweeted March 24, 2018 and garnered nearly 2,000 retweets and 3,800 likes. The creators of the GIF at *Gab* openly claimed it was supposed to be viewed as political satire/parody hours after the company tweeted the GIF (Mezzofiore, 2018).

It is especially ironic that such hateful expressions were directed at Gonzalez due to supposedly tearing up the US Constitution. Had she actually torn up a copy of the Constitution, this would be protected by free speech conventions. However, the perpetrator of the crime, Nikolas Cruz, commented on YouTube about wanting to be a professional school shooter. This was reported to the FBI, but was not followed up on due to the same First Amendment protections that would have permitted Gonzalez to tear up the Constitution as depicted in the hyperreal GIF produced by those who reject Gonzalez and what she represents. Had Cruz actually threatened a real person, that would be different, but since he allegedly threatened simply to kill people, that was permitted and largely ignored. Enter a young, bisexual, Cuban-American woman who chose to speak up about the problematic access to weapons such as the AR-15, itself representative of the influence the NRA has in politics, and the venomous memes followed accordingly.

Role of Metaphor: Procatoptric Staging

In terms of the semiotic suggestiveness of the Gonzalez GIF, its function closely resembles metaphor. According to Umberto Eco (1986), metaphors allow us to know more about the inserted items of knowledge than the schematic relation that is filled up. In other words, the remixing of the Gonzalez GIF to posit that she tore up the US Constitution speaks volumes about the people who identify with it, share it, post it, despite knowing or suspecting it to be a fake. In fact, one person associated with helping to make the GIF go viral, Adam Baldwin, an actor and conservative voice on Twitter with over 200,000 followers, claimed that he knew it was a doctored image but that it served the purpose of "political satire" (Danner, 2018). Again, to draw on Eco, these examples of remixing reality by making clips or images conform to specific ideological practice exemplifies Eco's articulation of *procatoptric staging*. Essentially, when a theatrical performance is staged, the audience is well informed that it is exactly that, a performance, and not a revelation of reality.

Eco (1986) claims that if we manipulate reality in any way, we also create ideology (p. 103). The staging of a theatrical performance which is mistaken as reality by an audience is the essence of what Eco describes as procatoptric staging (p. 219). To view the claim that Gonzalez tore up the Constitution (or to view the Cuban flag on her jacket as allegiance with a communist regime, thus implying further that '*they want to take our guns away*'...) is to see these claims as staged performances mistaken as real. Perhaps even worse as in the case of Baldwin, procatoptric staging means that people would know the images are fake but share them anyway in order to reify their own ideological practice.

To return to Eco's (1986) suggestion that the manipulation of reality is essentially the creation of ideology, this means the following: "we must select one property of a group – either a known or assumed property – and then we must affix it by proxy of choice to knowledge of the group" (p. 103). In this way, internet memes can be deployed strategically to reinforce identity using strong emotions (such as fear and hatred) to further a message – be it for the purpose of getting something to go viral or to cause confusion. The following section compares the implications of both cases.

Making Sense of It All

The *Babadook* meme offers glimpses into the construction of identity at least related to the LGBTQ+ community writ large. The Parkland tragedy and ensuing activism of the students were met online with memes that chastise and lampoon them and also that assign conspiratorial theories to them. This odd juxtaposition – between the positive progressiveness of *The Babadook* and the venom associated with the memes that attack the Parkland students – suggests one of possibly two conclusions. Could social media actually help ameliorate polarized tensions? Could it act as a kind of *hate outlet* whereby, similar to the cathartic theory in the larger video game and violence research narrative, participating in expressing hateful, angry, and frustrated views online actually produces a social good? On the other hand, could social media and all its fragmentation, algorithmic interplay, bots, etc. actually be responsible for exacerbating the situation, making nerves even more frayed, increasing anger, and justifying hateful slurs? It is perhaps best to view social media as a neutral, yet not an innocuous, force. It is one that can assist in ameliorating problematic issues but can also be a forum for fake news and hateful expressions.

Specifically, in terms of identity construction at least, the marking of difference – whether accomplished consciously, intentionally, or otherwise – is the determining factor in both instances. With *The Babadook* and related LGBTQ+ memes, the function is to visually announce support, for example, of an aspect related to sexual orientation in a largely heteronormative culture. However, when certain actions or voices are praised, then that which is not consonant with the projected identity is indirectly excluded. In the case of *The Babadook* and related LGBTQ+ issues, this may simply be reduced to *showing support means implicitly acknowledging judgmental views not welcome by the LGBTQ+ community*. This should not be controversial. However, looking at the memes leveraged by those who oppose Emma Gonzalez, a strikingly similar progression emerges. The important point here is that the marking of difference should be viewed as a neutral category in the process of identity construction. As individuals shared the *Babadook* meme, this practice within the community is a positive process. Similarly, as individuals shared Rep. Steve King's image-macro meme of Emma Gonzalez's use of the Cuban flag on her jacket or the viral spread of David Hogg-as-crisis-actor, this practice as well can be understood within that (or those) communities as an agreeable process Farhi (2018). In both instances, identity is recursively constituted and the struggle to build and sustain identity, once again to recall Giddens (1991), means that the process in both (possibly extreme) examples is essentially identical. It is within the discursive practice of deploying memes for such strategic purposes that identity is simultaneously permitted to flex itself, to adjust to new information, to evaluate it and to determine whether it fits within a view of the self. In this process of identity negotiation, constraining forces clearly also determine our choices due to desires such as how we want to be seen online, pressure to conform to the group, etc.

Meme-ing Ourselves to Death?

Finally, it is perhaps advisable to close with a reference to the work of Neil Postman. In his (1985) *Amusing Ourselves to Death*, Postman's central thesis was that a particular medium is only able to sustain a particular ideational niveau. Extending the media ecological argument of Marshall McLuhan, (i.e., media as an environment which we inhabit, and which invariably impacts us alongside our ability to influence media as well), Postman posits that television content, especially news, devolves into a commodified thing, something to consume at a base as opposed to an intellectual level. He cites how modern US presidents (though at the time he was referring to Ronald Reagan) are known more visually than what they say, or less still, than what they write when compared to the experience in the nineteenth century. The power of the soundbite also fuels the spectacle of commoditized content for consumption rather than speculation, discussion, debate, etc.

One can only surmise what Postman would say about the issues addressed in this chapter. The capacity for social media to allow for highly particularized groups and communities to articulate, circulate, spread, etc. ideas and arguments (often in the form of internet memes) serves to interpellate further the same individuals according to an ideological practice consonant with the given group, community, issue, and so on. Postman's thesis, when applied to social media in general but also to specific forms of communication permitted by the same media, suggests a dystopian view. Postman would likely also suggest caution in the deployment of memes, and in their reception. His analysis of US television showed audiences may form around content, presumably designed with the same audience in mind, as if the messages contained within are packaged neatly for each individual. Internet memes, in their assistance in the negotiation of identity, operate similarly.

Serious discussion and debate require informed individuals willing to review their own points of view, reevaluate when necessary, and to consider the points expressed by others with respect, despite a potential absence of agreement with said points. The viral spread of the Gonzalez GIF-as-internet meme on Twitter or the general vitriol directed at the Parkland students in the form of memes that oppose their efforts to propose a tenable gun control plan suggests a retreat to tribalism, a recoiling away from informed discussion and debate, and disavowal of the value of another's point of view, especially when it is accompanied by factual evidence.

Instead of encouraging social bonds, ameliorating tensions, decompressing frustration and anger, individuals can deploy internet memes as shadows of an assumed identity. Its ideological practice is manifested in the form of strict adherence to the values that constitute a particular group's sense of cohesion. Obviously, as in the case of the *Babadook* meme, as well as many others, internet memes can accomplish supportive if not also more generally, positive ends. However, this example is naturally rooted in the knowledge that such support is necessitated due to fears of marginalization and ostracization.

In closing, I wish to refer to the work of Timothy Snyder, the Richard C. Levin Professor of History at Yale University. In writing about the concerns stirred by the seemingly endless reign of Vladimir Putin, the surprise of the UK's Brexit vote, as well as the shocking electoral victory of Donald Trump in 2016, Snyder suggests that we are entering a period which he terms the *politics of eternity* (which is discussed in the chapter on political internet memes). Essentially, "the politics of eternity performs a masquerade of history, though a different one. It is concerned with the past, but in a self-absorbed way, freed from any real concern with facts" (Snyder, 2018, p. 121). Echoes of Postman's cynicism are present, and necessarily so. While Snyder is specifically talking of political movements, the use of internet memes in the construction of identity can also follow the same trajectory – the sense of being free from concern with facts permeates the polarized spaces in social media.

The tragedy in assuming, as Snyder does that "[p]ost-truth is prefascism" (2018, p. 71) is that we are not in an era where truth does not matter; rather, as I have argued elsewhere (Wiggins, 2017), our era is defined by malleable truth. The real horror of social media is that it can provide individuals with ways of constructing their own truths, facts, etc. to continue the resistance against engaging in any meaningful debate. Identity – fluid, unstable, defined by demarcation of difference, an example of a reflexive project, etc. – can thus be a liberating and constraining force but one that peddles in facts as well as falsity in the form of internet memes.

References

Butler, J. (1988). Performative acts and gender constitution: An essay in phenomenology and feminist theory. *Theatre Journal, 40*(4), 519–531.

Butler, J. (1990). *Gender trouble* (2nd ed.). New York: Routledge.

Butler, J. (2004). Sex, gender performativity, and the matter of bodies. In S. Salih (Ed.), *The Judith Butler reader* (pp. 19–138). Malden, MA: Blackwell Publishing.

Danner, C. (2018, March 25). People are sharing fake photos of Emma González tearing up the Constitution. *New York Magazine*. Retrieved from http://nymag.com/daily/intelligencer/2018/03/some-conservatives-are-sharing-a-fake-photo-of-emma-gonzalez.html

Eco, U. (1986). *Semiotics and the philosophy of language*. Bloomington: Indiana University Press.

Farhi, P. (2018, February 23). What is Gateway Pundit, the conspiracy-hawking site at the center of the bogus Florida 'crisis actors' hype? *The Washington Post: Style*. Retrieved from https://www.washingtonpost.com/lifestyle/style/what-is-gateway-pundit-the-conspiracy-hawking-site-at-the-center-of-the-bogus-florida-crisis-actors-hype/2018/02/23/dded562a-174e-11e8-b681-2d4d462a1921_story.html?noredirect=on&utm_term=.6889d920cf9a

Fraser, V. (2010). Queer closets and rainbow hyperlinks: The construction and constraint of queer subjectivities online. *Sexuality Research and Social Policy, 7*(1), 30–36.

Gibbs, A. (2013). Apparently unrelated: Affective resonance, concatenation and traumatic circuitry in the terrain of the everyday. In M. Atkinson & M. Richardson (Eds.), *Traumatic affect* (pp. 129–147). Newcastle upon Tyne: Cambridge Scholars.

Giddens, A. (1991). *Modernity and self-identity: Self and society in the late modern age.* Cambridge: Polity Press.

Goldman, A., & Mazzei, P. (2018, February 15). YouTube comment seen as early warning in shooting left little for F.B.I. to investigate. *The New York Times.* Retrieved from https://www.nytimes.com/2018/02/15/us/politics/nikolas-cruz-youtube-comment-fbi.html

Hillier, L., & Harrison, L. (2007). Building realities less limited than their own: Young people practising same-sex attraction on the internet. *Sexualities, 10*(1), 82–100.

Hunt, E. (2017, June 11). The Babadook: How the horror movie monster became a gay icon. *The Guardian.* Retrieved from https://www.theguardian.com/film/2017/jun/11/the-babadook-how-horror-movie-monster-became-a-gay-icon

Jenkins, H., Ito, M., & boyd, d. (2016). *Participatory culture in a networked era: A conversation on youth, learning, commerce, and politics.* Cambridge: Polity Press.

Laclau, E. (1977). *Politics and ideology in Marxist theory: Capitalism, fascism, populism.* London: New Left Books.

McDermott, E., Roen, K., & Piela, A. (2015). Explaining self-harm: Youth cybertalk and marginalized sexualities and genders. *Youth & Society, 47*(6), 873–889. doi:10.1177/0044118x13489142

Neal, D. J. (2018, February 28). Uber driver says Nikolas Cruz told her: 'I am going to my music class'. *Miami Herald.* Retrieved from http://www.miamiherald.com/news/local/community/broward/article202565414.html

Reed, J. (2018, February 21). Hate speech, atrocities, and fake news: the crisis of democracy in Myanmar. Financial Times. Retrieved from https://www.ft.com/content/2003d54e-169a-11e8-9376-4a6390addb44

Rubin, J. D., & McClelland, S. I. (2015). 'Even though it's a small checkbox, it's a big deal': stresses and strains of managing sexual identity(s) on Facebook. *Culture, Health, & Sexuality, 17*(4), 512–526. doi:10.1080/13691058.2014.994229

Scott, D. T. (2013). Refining 'resonance' as sympathetic intertextual relations: Pet Shop Boys score Battleship Potemkin. *Music, Sound, and the Moving Image, 7*(1), 53–82.

Scott, D. T. (2014). The empathetic meme: Situating Chris Crocker with the media history of LGBTQ+ equality struggles. *Journal of Communication Inquiry, 38*(4), 308–324.

Sit, R. (2018, March 26). More than 2 million in 90 per cent of voting districts joined *March for Our Lives* protests. *Newsweek.* Retrieved from http://www.newsweek.com/march-our-lives-how-many-2-million-90-voting-district-860841

Snyder, T. (2018). *The road to unfreedom: Russia, Europe, America.* London: Penguin Random House.

State, B., & Wernerfelt, N. (2015, October 15). America's coming out on Facebook. *Facebook Research.* Retrieved from https://research.fb.com/americas-coming-out-on-facebook

Vaidhyanathan, S. (2018). *Antisocial media: How Facebook disconnects us and undermines democracy.* New York: Oxford University Press.

Wiggins, B. E. (2017). Constructing malleable truths: Memes from the 2016 U.S. Presidential campaign. *Proceedings of the 4th Annual European Conference on Social Media.* Vilnius, Lithuania.

8 Internet Memes as a Form of...Art?

Internet meme creation and propagation involve innumerable aesthetic approaches, often leveraging a mundane image to offer critical commentary regarding a real-world issue. It is precisely this final point that defines the scope of this chapter. Furthermore, whether or to what degree an internet meme incorporates such structural approaches as collage, pastiche, bricolage, etc. these choices serve the discursive power of the meme in terms of the semiotic function of meaning-making.

The impetus of this chapter is to assert a conceptual connection between what is commonly called or understood to be *internet memes* and Dada and Surrealist art. Naturally not all internet memes share this conceptual link. My claim is those internet memes which inhere a critique of society, politics, gender, sexuality, etc. (i.e. those issues which tend to polarize people or which demarcate directionalities) contain a relationship to Dada and consequently must be discussed. A later section delves more deeply into this relationship, but for now I should emphasize that Dada and Surrealism were movements that are defined minimally as critical reactions to society rather than overt attempts to make or be art.

In this work thus far, I have defined internet memes by drawing on the work of others but also based on my own analytical view. In addition, I have argued that memes are best understood as visual arguments, and that the etymological root of *internet meme* should not be the Dawkinsian *mimema* but rather *enthymeme*, as noted in the first chapter. Additionally, I have proposed that ideological practice is situated within internet memes and is communicated, following my elaboration of Shifman's (2013) typology of memetic dimensions, with a reliance on the semiotic construction of meaning and intertextual references. Further, I have asserted that internet memes are a genre of online communication, and as such inhere three distinct traits as artifacts of digital culture, namely, virtual physicality, purposeful production and consumption, and social and cultural connection.

These contributions attest to the importance of the internet meme and related remix and viral media in digital culture. My activity in this regard proceeds not simply for the purpose of academic rumination but rather to demystify the meme in relation to the richness of its communicative capacity. Especially with reference to memes that share traits with Dada, the humorous and critical often merge and/or work in tandem.

My perspective differs somewhat from that of Phillips and Milner (2017) or Shifman (2013, 2014) in that while internet memes certainly operate also as a joke, they are clearly more dynamic that simple bon mot especially with respect to those memes criticizing a real-world issue, event, or person. The rationale to look backward, to look toward history comes from the sense that the discursive affordances provided by internet memes are not unique to the current digital moment. However, and justifiably so, Shifman (2014, p. 4) rather astutely points out that the pervasiveness of mediated communication represents a hyper-memetic discourse whereby "almost every major public event sprouts a stream of memes". It is increasingly difficult to discern the limits of what can be *memed* and/or what the future of memes may hold, whether and if they will remain a part of digital culture, and how they will change overtime.

Shifman (2013) notes that the internet meme is a kind of "conceptual troublemaker", one which defies singular categorization. I am afraid that I must add to the conceptual problematic by asserting that internet memes are indicative of an additional feature. Namely, internet memes, especially those concerned with communicating a critique – however obvious or implicit – represent a new cultural form of artistic expression. Internet memes are a form of art.

My rationale to explore historical linkages between memes and Dada and Surrealist art began in part in an analysis of the video *America First, the Netherlands Second*. The remixing of actual statements made by Donald Trump in the video accomplishes a critique of his rhetoric and ideology in a fashion similar in structure and intent in Dada and Surrealist art. This tendency is not unique to that meme; it is also present in other internet memes and indeed other forms of digital discourse (such as darkly humorous and distanced irony in viral videos, to be discussed in greater detail in another section). Before proceeding with a deeper discussion of Dada and Surrealism and also before the analysis of the *America First, the Netherlands Second* video, it is worthwhile to consider related forms of cultural criticism produced in such a way for mass consumption – again similar in form and purpose to (critical) internet memes. Following this, I will discuss selected popular internet memes from 2016 to 2017 and analyze them according to my elaboration of the model originally introduced by Shifman (2013). My elaboration of the model considers the absence of human speech and elevates the importance of semiotics and intertextuality in the expression of ideological practice.

The Bizarre, Absurd, Cringeworthy, Ironic, etc. as Expressions of Disillusionment

The practice of taking available content and remixing it for critical observation is demonstrated in the following diverse range of examples. As an initial example, the video parody of television genres known as *Too Many Cooks* serves this purpose well. The *Too Many Cooks* video was published on the Adult Swim YouTube channel in November 2014 and is perhaps best described as merging absurd and surreal approaches to humor. This is accomplished through repetition and a structural absurdist component of constantly changing the expected outcome through internal remix, redirection, and elevation of the surreal to exaggerate the exaggerated. It is perhaps best to view the video clip for one's own interpretation, but it bears mentioning that viral videos in general rarely *go viral* if they are long, that is more than three or four minutes (Nahon & Hemsely, 2013). The *Two Many Cooks* video broke that rule with its running time of just over 11 minutes. At the current estimate of this writing, the video has over 16 million views and over 200,000 likes.

Further, such bizarre and absurd creations like the *How to Basic* YouTube channel, David Lewandowski's videos (check out *late for meeting* or *going to the store*), the series of *We'll Be Right Back* video memes, the *What does the fox say?* music video, the *Pen Pineapple Pen* video (which currently has over 240 million views since it was uploaded in November 2016), the *Eric Andre Show* or videos posted to YouTube by Poppy all inhere a deeply ironic and often darkly humorous stance. Poppy's videos are especially cringeworthy but offer a peculiar reflection of the modern age. In particular, Poppy's video entitled *Am I ok?* speaks to insecurities and anxieties consonant with current times. Her choice to call herself *Poppy* appears to be an explicit reference to Pop Art which arguably developed out of Abstract Expressionism and neo-Dada. Indeed, her first video, *Poppy Eats Cotton Candy*, is highly suggestive of Danish filmmaker Jørgen Leth's film *Andy Warhol Eats a Hamburger* (Open Culture, 2018). Warhol summed up his purpose saying that,

> [w]hat's great about this country is that America started the tradition where the richest consumers buy essentially the same things as the poorest. You can be watching TV and see Coca-Cola, and you know that the President drinks Coke, Liz Taylor drinks Coke, and just think, you can drink Coke too. A Coke is a Coke and no amount of money can get you a better Coke than the one the bum on the corner is drinking.
>
> (Horwitz, 2001, p. 229)

Perhaps, this is no truer in modern times with a former reality TV show star, real estate mogul, and billionaire Donald Trump as the US

President who is known for his consumption of fast food (Jacobs & Pettypiece, 2018).

In all of the aforementioned examples irony, alongside other emotions and forms of expression, appears to be paramount to the formation and reception of the message. Of course, the opportunity to appreciate such expressions as ironic, bizarre, etc. depends on the ability to interpret them in such a way. For my purposes, I take the position that in the previous examples, be they *Too Many Cooks*, the *Eric Andre Show* memes, or the connection between Andy Warhol and Poppy, irony is essential in this form of communication.

Interestingly, one of the individuals closely connected to the spirit (but not the dogma) of Dada is Marcel Duchamp who said that "[his] irony is that of indifference: meta-irony" (Sanouillet & Peterson, 1973, p. 6). In what follows, the sense of meta-irony, dark humor, and absurdist perspectives permeates the examples both representative of Dada and Surrealism as well as the internet memes included for comparison.

As a developing form of artistic expression internet memes exemplify digital culture especially because of the public sphere in which they are produced and shared. In this way, internet memes function as a kind of *Gesamtkunstwerk*, or *total work of art* which "required the collaboration of the public" (Richter, 1965, p. 213). Accordingly, taking part in a memetic spectacle – in the creation or curation of internet memes regarding a particular real-world event or issue – is perhaps reducible to the simple sentiment that *'the world is crazy but at least we can make memes'*. This is the sentiment that ultimately links early Dada and related artistic expression to the internet meme of the twenty-first century.

Deploying memes and related digital content to express dark irony, absurdist perspectives, and/or a general disillusionment with the modern age connects directly with the motivations in the Dada and Surrealist movement. The dark humor consonant with internet memes and Dadaism demonstrates the *degree* of the disillusionment. Writing in the blog *Medium*, Megan Hoins (2016) claims that, from an American perspective,

> we were promised to be whoever we wanted to be, and we were given high unemployment rates and no guarantee of a job after college...[we] were promised peace and prosperity, and we were handed terrorism and a severe economic recession.

And that was before Brexit, the rise of far-right political parties in Europe, bellicose rhetoric regarding Iran and North Korea, before the spread of the *incel* (or involuntarily celibate) movement, before the #unitetheright neo-Nazi rally in Virginia, before Facebook colluded with Cambridge Analytica (Lewis & Hilder, 2018), before #metoo and resulting backlash (Tan & Porzecanski, 2018), before Russian interference in political campaigns, and of course, before Trump became the President of the USA. While I do not wish to imply a political preference, my emphasis is on the occurrence of social and political upheaval in a relatively short amount of time. Accordingly, internet memes coalesce as a fitting form of expression during such times. Generationally, it may be the confluence of an increasingly mediated lifestyle alongside a need to express oneself in a world rife with disillusionment that makes memes salient with millennials, especially those memes with a deeply ironic, darkly humorous, absurdist, etc. stance. The next sections deliver background on Dada before proceeding with the remaining analysis and discussion.

Dada, Surrealism, and Internet Memes

Dada was an art and literary movement which began in Zürich in 1916 during the brutal realities of the First World War, then known as The Great War. The earliest individuals associated with Dada assembled at Café Voltaire in Zürich and used the venue to express their indignation and horror at the outbreak of war around them. Tristan Tzara, Hugo Ball, Richard Huelsenbeck, Hans Richter, and others formed the nucleus of nascent Dada. They perceived the war happening outside of neutral Switzerland as a failure of the values and attitudes enjoyed by a civilized society which had descended into the worst conflict the world had witnessed up to that point in time. Dada artists expressed their disillusionment with the social values that precipitated the war and employed groundbreaking methods of artistic expression in order "to expose accepted and often repressive conventions of order and logic by shocking people into self-awareness" (MoMA, 2018). The lesson to be gained from my comparison of structural as well as thematic components found in Dada and internet memes is to propose that the use of dark and distanced irony is not necessarily unique to the current moment. However, and with respect to the affordances provided by smart phones, tablets, apps, etc., the ability for large numbers of people to take part in such expressions is endemic to the modern age and unlike anything before or during the Dada and related movements.

In digital culture, a tendency exists to discuss modern life through invocation and citation of the ironic, satirical, profane, dark and/or offensive humor, etc. in order to make sense of the world – just like the Dadaists and surrealists in the early twentieth century. Milner's (2013) concept known as the "logic of lulz", or the approach that the internet meme often may incorporate a "distanced irony" is a similar sentiment. However, and with respect to the expanding research on internet memes as signposts of digital culture, the confluence of irony, dark humor, disillusionment, etc. within memes suggests perhaps much more than "distanced irony". In fact, conceptually, "distanced" is negated by the black mirrors individuals peer into in search of information, connection, distraction, etc. What is offered by the "logic of lulz" is situated in contemporary times and as such lacks the benefits gained by considering earlier and similar modes of expressions commensurate with the degree of disillusionment.

Structural Similarities between Dada and Internet Memes

Structurally, Dadaist and Surrealist art often used text and photography specifically to demonstrate a complex and ironic engagement with the issues of life during the war and in the time before the Second World War (Hopkins, 2004). Several key examples of Dada and Surrealist artwork help to clarify the connection between them and internet memes, both structurally and thematically. In a cut-and-pasted print, Dadaist Johannes Baader sought to parody the military elite in 1920s Germany. The print, known as *The Author of the Book Fourteen Letters of Christ in His Home (Der Verfasser das Buches Vierzehn Briefe Christi in seinem Heim)*, is a photomontage and shows a room in what appears to be a home. A central figure (actually Baader himself) was removed by cutting it out of the photograph and laying over an image of a mannequin in military attire. This deliberate process of creating a visual statement, or argument (namely that the German military deserves to be mocked), through cutting and pasting fragments of other material, is a structural component definitive of internet memes. Consider the deployment of the so-called *Pepper Spray Cop* meme or the Kayne West-inspired *Imma let you finish* or *Kanye Interrupts* meme. In many of the iterations of either meme, an image of the pepper-spraying cop or Kanye West is inserted into another context (DaVinci's *The Last Supper* or the sinking of the Titanic) for the purpose of parody, critiquing police authority (in the case of the pepper spray cop) or the detachment of celebrity (in the case of Kanye West). Consider also the *White Woman Calls the Cops* meme as discussed in Chapter 6. This is clearly a critical-ironic deployment of discursive practice, one which necessitates humor to operate critically.

A further example of structural similarity between Dada and internet memes is found in Max Ernst's *Santa Conversazione* (1921). Ernst constructed collages made from "recognizable imagery, juxtaposing fragments of encyclopedia plates, commercial catalogs, anatomical treatises and photographs to produce disturbing counter-realities" (Hopkins, 2004, p. 74). With regard to semiotic and intertextual choices, internet memes are constructed in a similar fashion. The so-called *Trump Executive Order* meme offers a fine example for comparison.

The meme shows the US president in a short video or GIF opening a folder which holds an executive order freshly signed by Trump. However, users removed the text of the executive order and filled in the white space with alternative text or child-like drawings. The looping video functions as a *visual soundbite*: users take an official moment and subtract the gravitas through the inserted text or drawing. Similar to Ernst's approach, users take available video and exaggerate the exaggerated. Ernst created a counter-reality, and similar to the work of Magritte and Dalí, criticized the real world through juxtaposing and remixing elements common to a known expectation. The Trump meme offers a conduit for the expression of similar sentimentality.

As noted in the introduction to this chapter, practices such as photomontage, collage, bricolage, etc. are conceptually similar to the visual construction of internet memes. As an early example in Dada, the practice of photomontage in Berlin, such as Hannah Höch's *Bourgeois Wedding Couple – Quarrel* (1919), functions as a critique of modern society by incorporating available pieces of print media to construct a parody of marriage. This process of collage or bricolage to create a new meaning from available pieces is central to the role of remix in internet memes. Situated in the context of discursive practice, individuals share internet memes to make fun of or criticize an issue or person but do so by assembling new patterns of meaning from available media. Whereas the Dadaist approach sought to undermine what was understood as art, and to encourage discussion of what constitutes art, the approach in internet memes to use dark humor and distanced irony to convey meaning often requires the incorporation of intertextual references. Such assembling represents one major feature of viewing internet memes as a new form of art.

Marcel Duchamp and the *Readymade*

One of the earliest Dadaists, Marcel Duchamp, introduced what he called the *readymade*, which was a mass-produced, prefabricated object, such as a window, a shovel, or a bicycle wheel but presented as art (Dabringer, Figlhuber, & Guserl, 2015; Hopkins, 2004). Duchamp (1961) notes that the function of the *readymade* is to demonstrate that "[a]n ordinary object [could be] elevated to the dignity of a work of art by the mere choice of an artist" (para. 2). Furthermore, the *readymade* challenged the notion that art had to be (dogmatically) beautiful.

Perhaps even more importantly, the *readymade* demonstrated that art could be removed from the aesthetic world thus negating the act of producing something and elevating the act of choosing and presenting as the definitive feature of an artist. Functionally, the *readymade* seeks to "collapse the distinction between art and non-art" (Hopkins, 2004, p. 98). Considering the degree of remix, photographic manipulation, juxtaposition, and the ease by which internet memes are shared and reproducible, it is helpful to view the internet meme as a digital *readymade*. Even though Duchamp disliked reproduction and second-hand experience, conceptually his *readymade* offers a clear pre-digital counterpart to the internet meme favored by disillusioned individuals.

As such the meme-as-digital-readymade seeks to collapse the distinction between reality and alternative reality, truth and fantasy, critique and joke. The more darkly connotative the internet meme, the more of a relationship it has with the impetus behind Dada and also Surrealist art approaches. While not discussing this relationship, Milner (2012) found that in politically critical internet memes that positioned President Barak Obama in a racist light, the dark connotation inheres an interdiscursive component making them powerful. Such memes are evidence of pop savviness in the production of more explicit political commentary.

Similarly, the function of the readymade as a mass-produced object was in its capacity to shock the viewer initially, to provide a jarring experience leading an individual to question the boundaries of art in consumerist, industrial society. The tendency within digital culture to mash-up and *poach* content (per Jenkins, 2012) pairs well with the intention of the readymade. However, the degree to which a meme may shock (as was intended by Duchamp's readymade) depends on its semiotic and intertextual construction as well as its decoded reception.

The function of the *readymade* was not to evoke dark sarcasm or irony but to critique assumptions of artistic convention. This approach shares the tendency of digital culture to mash-up content for discursive purposes, regardless of the surface joke or subject-matter contained within.

Internet Memes and Literary Linkages: *Neue Sachlichkeit*

Additionally, linkages between the essence of expression in internet memes and Dadaism is also found in literary theory. In Walter Benjamin's classic text *The Work of Art in the Age of Mechanical Reproduction*, he suggests that "Dadaism attempted to create by pictorial – and literary – means the effects which the public today seeks in the film" (1969/1935, p. 16). Here, he highlights how Dadaism started in one form and resonated with audiences such as to cause a yearning for related forms of expression in other media, such as film. This is the same case with internet memes. Benjamin also writes that the work of the Dadaists "hit the spectator like a bullet, it happened to him, thus acquiring a tactile quality" (p. 17). This suggests a helpful linkage to my deliberation on the etymological root of internet meme to be *enthymeme* rather than *mimema* as preferred by Dawkins. Similar to the work that emerged from Dada and the Surrealists, as well as perhaps art in general, the individual viewing or experiencing the work has to fill in something in order to 'get' the critique, in order to understand the argument.

Dada and Surrealist motivations centered around skepticism of society in general and emphasized human isolation through industrial incursion into social spheres. The German literary and art movement known as *Neue Sachlichkeit,* or "new objectivity", offered a way to represent an issue by showing both the external and internal parts, such as the ways sexuality and the feminine are articulated in a film like *Mädchen in Uniform* (McCormick, 2009, p. 275). This tendency to show the internal and external parts of an issue is also present in many sub-genres of internet meme.

Artists producing work representative of *Neue Sachlichkeit* tendencies highlighted social and political turmoil of life as expressed in paintings which included characters such as war-profiteers, beggars, prostitutes, etc. and explored the rise of the metropolis. Artists such as Otto Dix and Georg Grosz reveled in the spectacle of the freedoms and sexual liberation granted by the changing social order but also acknowledged increased alienation from nature and rural life.

An example demonstrates the dichotomy of the *internal* and *external* as applied to internet memes. Namely, a two-panel image-based meme emerged after the so-called *spiderman* incident in France in 2018, in which a Malian immigrant, Mamoudou Gassama, climbed the balconies of an apartment building to save a dangling infant. Shown in Figure 8.1, internally the meme shows a cartoon version of the heroic act, which was awarded by French President Emmanuel Macron with French citizenship. Externally, the same act is juxtaposed with the darkly ironic and detached notions of other immigrants wishing to be accepted within the European Union. The meme accomplishes this with no text, except with the semiotic insertion of a green check mark to indicate proper behavior (saving the child, risking one's life) and a red X to demonstrate undesired behavior (trying to scale a fence metaphorically representative of immigration policy in the European Union).

It is important to note that the attributes *internal* and *external* refer two specific semiotic functions of the meme with respect to its real-world referent and real-world critique (and consequently expression of ideological practice). *Internal* refers first to the event or the media spectacle which encouraged transformation into the digital discursive unit shared online as memes. *External* refers to the larger situation which the semiotic function of the meme finally signifies. The same relationship between *internal/external* can be applied to internet memes which inhere some degree of thematic dichotomy especially when it references at least two or more ways of seeing a real-world phenomenon.

René Magritte and *The Treachery of Images* (or *La trahison des images*)

It is important to note that Surrealism grew out of Dadaism and rejected the idea of civilization and emphasized or questioned unconsciousness, chance, sexuality, and taboo. This is especially evident in the work of Miró, Dalí, and others. Surrealist painter Joan Miró used an *automatic* approach "which was characterized by this kind of capricious poetic

Figure 8.1 Remixing the French *Spiderman.*

transformation with visual signs undergoing continual metamorphosis" (Hopkins, 2004, p. 80). Additionally, Salvador Dalí and Rene Magritte intentionally used double-images as in Magritte's *Le Viol* (the rape, 1934) and Dalí's *Paranoiac Face* (1931) for the purpose of discrediting reality. Furthermore, American art historian Rosalind Krauss claimed that especially in the photographic manipulation of Man Ray and Maurice Tabard "the reality which the mechanical nature of photography ostensibly records is inherently unstable: merely a collection of movable signs, like a text" (Hopkins, 2004, p. 85). These disparate examples demonstrate that efforts within Dadaism and Surrealism to make meaning echo the capacity within internet memes to communicate an ideological practice in a similar way. Especially with the emphasis on disillusionment, internet memes are excellent vehicles for social and cultural expression.

It is helpful to consider the surrealist work of Magritte with regard to images in general but more specifically as this discussion relates to internet memes and the function of the image-as-representation across meme sub-genres. Generally speaking, Magritte's efforts served to elevate and emphasize confusion and often employed obstructions (such as an apple in front of a face) in his other works. In *The Treachery of Images*, it is *representation* which is emphasized, and Magritte's argument in the painting may be obvious, namely that the painting of a pipe is clearly not a pipe. However, his point goes a bit further: if a person is shown a photo of an object or person, such as a piece of fruit or a famous celebrity, it is highly likely that the person may say that the image is in fact the thing represented. Here, Magritte critiques language; the assumption of the painting lies in the essentialist tradition of thought, at least with regard to identity and identifying things and people, that objects have an essential, knowable and true signification. However, the point is that the words ascribed to objects are arbitrary.

Magritte intended to illustrate three points in his *The Treachery of Images*. His use of the pipe is to illustrate that it is, of course, not really a pipe but a representation. Also, the words announcing the image are supposed to have a relationship with the image (which the viewer makes possible, similar to the process of the enthymeme). Perhaps most importantly, the relationship between object and representation can be *corrupted* by language. However, the trick is that we are unaware of the manipulation of meaning and representation, unaware of the ways in which language controls expectation.

In internet memes, and with deliberate emphasis on semiotics, the image and assignment of meaning has taken a new form. A represented thing online may not mean what you think and how it was constructed is exactly that, a construction, which is nuanced by media narratives, themselves and construction. In *getting the joke* (or the often superficial yet socially salient point of a meme, especially socio-culturally and/or political critical ones), a person is ensconced within ideology.

What Magritte produced is something to be studied, mused upon, discussed, etc. because we know that is the intention. However, with internet memes, the same play on language, representation, and meaning occur. Due to the rapidity by which the hypermemetic procession of images saturate online spaces, we succumb to their surface meaning and possibly fail to grasp the power of memes with respect to the maintenance of ideological practice. Before proceeding with the analysis of the *America First, Netherlands Second* video memes, I wish to point out that, perhaps the ultimate horror is that we begin to realize the manner by which memes help to preserve and reconstitute ideological practice but that we continue doing so regardless of the enlightened awareness.

Introducing a Neo-Dadaist Semiotic

Drawing on Dada and Surrealism has provided the foundation for a *neo-Dadaist semiotic*. Accordingly, this term is perhaps best understood as a *millennial* neo-Dadaist semiotic, given that much of the internet memes and related viral media which are thematically related are produced, shared, and consumed by millennials. Regardless of the millennial component, a *neo-Dadaist semiotic* is characterized by the following, in no particular order: dark humor; distanced irony; disillusionment; horror/shock at the modern age (but with no direct or explicit deliberation on that which horrifies or shocks); bizarre and absurd expressions; self-deprecation; cringe; offensive humor; scatological references.

The purpose of the first part of the analysis, namely the discussion of *America First, the Netherlands Second* is to explore the neo-Dadaist semiotic in terms of a video. What follows is an extended look at popular memes of 2016–2017 which are analyzed in terms of my elaboration of the model with specific reference to the lack of human speech.

America First, Netherlands Second: *The Most Fantastic, Absolutely Tremendous Analysis, Really. It's Great*

Following the inauguration of Donald Trump, a comedic sketch on a Dutch TV show called *Zondag met Lubach* uploaded a response to the new president's clarion call to focus on *America First*. The video quickly achieved virality and also inspired other countries in addition to iterations belonging to the so-called *reaction* video genre to join in the parodic fun by creating versions echoing the satirical sentiment in the original video. Table 8.1 shows the analysis of *America First, the Netherlands Second* following Shifman's model.

Most if not all of the videos in the *Netherlands Second* genre include some type of personal message introducing itself to Donald Trump, as if speaking to him personally. The original video and several subsequent remixes also employ a voice-over impersonating Trump. Saturating the videos is a tendency toward dichotomous reasoning with an emphasis on extremes. This echoes Trump's own rhetorical style, which favors short sentences, few polysyllabic words, and embellishing language demonstrated through the use of words and phrases such as *great, big, tremendous, huge, fantastic,* and repetitions of such key words as if to exaggerate the superlative. This use of language positions the subject as being of paramount importance to the USA with other countries denoted

Table 8.1 *America First, Netherlands Second*: Content, Form, and Stance

Iteration	Views	Content	Form	Stance
America First, Netherlands Second (NS)	23 M	Mocking Netherlands through Trump's rhetoric; Echoing Trump's own words	Trump-like voiceover; montage-video, short clips, occasional direct references between voiceover and video; official looking title shot; 4 min 05 s	Affected voice, parody of Trump; hyperbole; Funny and mocking keying; referential and conative

as *the worst, scumbags, losers, total failures,* etc. Thus, the juxtaposition of good and bad delivers a polarized and quintessentially Trumpian view of the world expressed in extremes.

The video largely adheres to real-world references to actual Trump statements, policies, implications, or remixes thereof. Consider the following segment from the original video:

> We've got Ponypark Slagharen, which is got to be the best ponypark in the world. It's true. They're the best pony's, they are. You can ride them. You can date them, you can grab'em by the pony, it's fantastic.
> (Transcript, 2017)

This is funny on the one hand because talking about a pony park using Trump's rhetorical style has a certain humorous effect, perhaps due to the absurdity of the subject matter. Yet, this excerpt embraces one of the most controversial aspects of Trump's character that emerged before the actual election in November 2016, in which an audio file from *Access Hollywood Live* featured Trump stating that as a celebrity he can have his way with women and can "grab 'em by the pussy" if he so chooses. In the *Netherlands Second* meme, the realness of the offensive nature of Trump's acquiescence with misogyny and sexual assault is remixed by the insertion of *pony* as a catachresis for what Trump actually said.

The *semiotics* of this style suggests a need to appeal to dark humor and to elevate the absurd in order to come to terms with the disillusionment and/or failure to accept the status quo in the modern age. Consider the following additional excerpt from the *Netherlands Second* video:

> In December we've got this scandalous tradition of Black Pete. It's the most offensive, the most racist thing you've ever seen. You'll love it, it's great. We also have a disabled politician for you to make fun of. Her name is Jetta Klijnsma. She is from the ministry of Silly Walks. You can do a great impersonation of her. Can't wait to see it.
> (Transcript, 2017)

The first specific reason why this excerpt embraces a neo-Dadaist semiotic is its explicit deployment of racism alongside the acknowledgement of Trump's racist leanings (such as his failure to disavow support from former KKK-leader David Duke, not to mention overt racist, misogynist, and homophobic content associated with Breitbart and Infowars, two news agencies close to Trump, among other examples). The excerpt also offers an internal criticism of an aspect of real Dutch culture, namely the Black Pete, or Zwarte Piet, celebration on December 5. The celebration involves the use of blackface and has been the subject of controversy (Criado, 2014; de Telegraaf, 2013).

In particular, the elevation of the hurtful, offensive, etc. to the humorous is not a reversal or even an acceptance of such views. Rather, it cathartically cleanses the more revolting aspects of Trump's platform through the use of humor as a way for people to share a laugh while also realizing the disillusionment they share in the face of the Trump presidency. Second, the casual reference to a disabled politician for the purpose of mocking her, itself a reference to the time when Trump publicly mocked a journalist with arthrogryposis, a congenital condition affecting the joints (Crilly, 2015), would normally seem offensive and discriminatory.

Instead, and true with reference to the neo-Dadaist semiotic, this is a move that transcends the *hyperreal* and moves toward the *real*: by referencing an actual action in which Trump mocked a disabled person, satire or parody fails because the realness of the world is shocking enough. Baudrillard explained that his term *hyperreal* is dominated by the circulation of fictions and signs (symbols, meaning, etc.) that have no referent, origin, or meaning. His recommended inoculation against the hyperreal is to inject the real into the hyperreal. The *Netherlands Second* meme accomplishes this precisely because it does not have to create new content per se, it does not need to make outrageous claims about Trump because he is outrageous. Simply by presenting his own perspectives or remixing his own words, semiotic meaning is reified through the insertion of real references to shocking behavior presented as sublime and enjoyable due to a shared disillusionment with the modern condition.

A Neo-Dadaist Semiotic in Image-Based Internet Memes

For the purpose of challenging my own argument and claim of a conceptual connection between internet memes and Dadaism, as well as related forms of artistic expression, I have conducted a series of Google searches for '*top memes of...*' for the years 2016 and 2017. In the course of my research, both toward this and previous works I have come to realize that with internet memes, it is important to have a kind of *felt sense*, meaning that it is crucial to be able to step back, and consider what the big picture is, to see beyond the humor of the initial moment, to view a particular meme, its iteration, or even a series of memes as a discourse and not simple bon mot. Accordingly, we can say that a meme has entered the mainstream when it has achieved a degree of virality which should be understood less in terms of a quantifiable number of likes, shares, reactions, retweets, etc. but rather virality in the sense of massive ideational spread endemic to a particular issue and achieving resonance with individuals and groups for specific reasons. Additionally, my intention is to close this chapter and indeed this book by testing my claim, both in elaborating Shifman's (2013) model but also, and perhaps more importantly, to demonstrate specific examples in situ of a neo-Dadaist semiotic.

Analyzing them with the elaboration of the model reveals the importance of semiotics and intertextuality in the dissemination of memes – whether merely for *fun* or also as an expression of ideological practice.

For practical reasons, I do not include all so-called *popular* memes from the years mentioned for this analysis. Rather, the selected memes represent the most commonly occurring memes assembled by outside parties as representative of *popular* memes for a given year. The included memes are shown in Table 8.2 below, and for impartiality they are listed in alphabetical order.

For the purpose of time, *Pepe the Frog*, *The Babadook*, and *Distracted Boyfriend* have all been discussed in previous chapters yet their relevance to this discussion is also pertinent. As part of this analysis, it is helpful to illustrate visually the point of orientation of the memes from 2016 and 2017. I have plotted all 20 memes in a qualitative coordinate plane in which its X or horizontal axis is political ideology understood as left-leaning and right-leaning and its Y or vertical axis emphasizes the *primary purpose* of the meme as being humorous or critical in nature, shown in Figure 8.2. Memes in *italics* are those from 2016 and underlined text represents memes from 2017.

The qualitative coordinate plane is based on an assessment of the meme's entrance into digital discourse and the ways in which it was deployed. However, several issues must be addressed before proceeding with the analysis and concluding discussion. One major limitation to this approach is my own subjectivity. While I can claim objectivity by establishing a reliable coding strategy that is consistent and also valid, since this deals with language and interpreting memes-as-texts I must admit that this approach is also purely descriptive; in the table I have attempted to plot the memes according to my interpretation of their original meaning based on '*what is there*' but not *why* it is there. Additionally, this analysis is limited in that the observations demonstrated

Table 8.2 Popular Memes from 2016 to 2017

2016	2017
1. Arthur's Clenched Fist	1. The Babadook
2. Bernie or Hillary	2. Covfefe
3. Confused Mr. Krabs	3. Distracted Boyfriend
4. Evil Kermit	4. Kendall Jenner, Pepsi
5. Fully Automated Luxury Gay Space Communism	5. Nothing but Respect for My President
6. Harambe	6. Roll Safe
7. Me at the Beginning/End of 2016	7. Salt Bae
8. Nut Button	8. The Floor is...
9. Pepe the Frog	9. This is the Future Liberals Want
10. Petty Joe Biden	10. White Guy Blinking

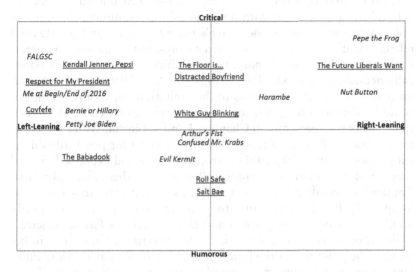

Figure 8.2 Qualitative Coordinate Plane for Plotting Memes: Political Ideology
and Primary Purpose.

in the table may not be an accurate reflection of reality. As an example from both ends of the political spectrum included in the coordinate plane, *Me at the Beginning/End of 2016* and *Pepe the Frog* each address specific ideological practices remixed through the inclusion of semiotic and intertextual choices. On the left-leaning side, *Me at the Beginning/ End of 2016* is clearly a political-cultural-critical message that expresses dismay, exhaustion, and disillusionment at the tumult that came to define 2016, namely the unexpected electoral victory of Donald Trump. Accordingly, I do not assume that people sharing this meme or participating in its further iterations are necessarily left-leaning politically, but the message articulated by the meme is left-leaning given the nature of its critique. Similarly, the *Pepe the Frog* meme is a good example of ideological practice on the political right given its deployment in 2016 and into 2017 especially by supporters of Trump. In fact, it is worth mentioning that it has evolved since its creator, artist Matt Furie, developed the comic character in 2005 and who intended it to be rather innocuous as opposed to its current use by alt-right, white supremacist, and neo-Nazi groups (McCausland, 2017). With regard to the limitation I mentioned, both these memes could be changed, modified, etc. to be more humorous or critical, and the political orientation could also be adjusted yet it is the original impetus for the meme which I plot, not necessarily the derivatives. In a sense, I am evaluating the ideational aspect of the discursive: these memes represent at their core a slightly flexible idea whose deployment is nuanced by mixing humor with some degree of visual argument. The interpretation of each meme is inescapably subjective; however, with my emphasis on examining the ideological practice indicated in the meme's use of semiotic and intertextual references, it is my sincere intention to present this analysis as objectively as possible. Furthermore, memes which I have plotted as politically neutral, such as *Salt Bae*, *Arthur's Fist*, or *Distracted Boyfriend*, must also be addressed in terms of the limitation. Each of those memes could be deployed for politically critical purposes on either the left or right side of the spectrum. In Chapters 3 and 4, I included an example of the *Distracted Boyfriend* meme posted to Twitter for politically different purposes. One critiqued the European Union and expressed implied support of an Italian exit similar to Brexit. The other criticized former Catalonian president Carles Puigdemont in his attempt to avoid arrest in Spain by fleeing to Belgium (the charges have since been dropped). Similarly, one could easily remix *Salt Bae* or *Arthur's Fist* to criticize a political perspective on either side of the spectrum or anywhere in between. The point is that the function of the remixed semiotic and intertextual choices in many image-based memes can be replaced at will and perceived in particular ways by specific groups of people with a shared opinion or perspective, but one which is unavoidably influenced by external media narratives. This is the *discursive power* of internet memes but one that is also dependent upon agency.

One meme in particular, *This is the Future Liberals Want*, must be clarified as I plot it as right-leaning and critical, but it underwent change as a meme. It started as an image posted by a far-right user to Twitter in May 2017. The original image features a photo of a woman in a niqab sitting next to a drag queen. However, the ensuing *responses* to the meme remixed it critically by '*owning*' the original message in the form of critique. While the meme originally started on the politically right side and with a critical purpose, its derivatives upended this message through satire, parody, mocking, and juxtaposition.

Analysis: Using the Elaboration of the Model

From Shifman's (2013) original introduction of her memetic typology, she asserts that an analysis of memes can be accomplished by addressing *content*, *form*, and *stance*. As I noted in the first chapter, due to the absence of human speech in image-based memes, *stance* is the location of semiotic and intertextual meaning. As a first step, I address those memes which I plotted near the center of the coordinate plane. Starting with the memes from 2016, *Arthur's Fist*, *Confused Mr. Krabs*, and even *Evil Kermit* are all plotted rather neutrally due to the flexibility of their deployment. For example, *Arthur's Fist* is taken from a screen capture of the character *Arthur* from the eponymous children's series but is used as a reaction-image meme. As such its deployment could be tinged with a politically left- or right-leaning message, depending on other inserted information. The benefit of examining stance with an emphasis on semiotics and intertextuality means realizing that a meme can be relatively neutral but, and here I feel the need to reiterate my point of Duchamp's *readymade*, once selected by digital culture to address an issue or concern, the *meaning* is altered. Similarly, the centrally plotted memes from 2017 also largely depend on inserted information for determining a political message. For example, *Salt Bae, White Guy Blinking, Roll Safe, The Floor is...*, and *Distracted Boyfriend* do not in and of themselves address a political perspective, left or right, but with the insertion of intertextual references and using semiotic tools such as metonymy or metaphor the meme can quickly become politically left- or right-leaning. I plotted *Harambe* as somewhat right-of-center, and this needs to be addressed. To clarify, *Harambe* was a 17-year-old silverback gorilla who was killed at the Cincinnati Zoo in late May 2016 to protect a child who had fallen into his enclosure (Knowyourmeme.com, 2016a). Amidst a flurry of memetic variations, such as including *Harambe* in homages to deceased celebrities such as David Bowie and Prince, the *Harambe* meme also attracted racist deployment in linking the deceased gorilla to African Americans, an association found to be common among whites in a series of psychological experiments (Goff, Eberhardt, Williams, & Jackson, 2008). Additionally, the *Harambe* meme developed into fodder for fake news as a means to explain Trump's surprise electoral victory. Specifically, several Twitter users posted that 11,000 or more people chose to write-in Harambe, the gorilla, as an alternative to Trump or Clinton. Consistent with fake news, however, even reporting that it was a fake is still communicating about it. For these two reasons, racist associations of African Americans and gorillas and the development of *Harambe* into fake news suggest more of a right-of-center lean.

For the memes which I have plotted with a discernibly left or right political lean, semiotics and intertextual reference still, of course, significantly impact meaning-making but the directionality of the message is already largely established, unlike the centrally/neutrally located memes addressed above. For example, the *Bernie or Hillary* meme started by poking fun, critically, at then-candidate Hillary Clinton in 2016 by positioning her as uncool, someone who is just trying to be cool but is not. With each subsequent remix, Bernie Sanders was positioned as proportionately cooler and hipper than Hillary but in an authentic and meaningful way. Clearly, this meme is left-leaning politically, and the intertextual references to popular culture communicated a sense of cool with regard to Bernie and uncool about Hillary. This accomplished an associative construction of Bernie Sanders as metaphorically cool and socially salient; in terms of ideological practice, the individuals who identified with this interpretation were more likely to receive the dominant meaning and share it accordingly. The juxtaposition of cool/uncool signifies a constructive semiotic approach.

With respect to a neo-Dadaist semiotic, it is necessary to identify which memes contain such communicative structures and how these are identifiable. Further, I believe it prudent to show the structural aspects of this approach in terms of its impact on the intended (or dominant) meaning of the meme as a text. As I have noted, several of the memes tend toward the neutral center, even those which may gravitate more toward a humorous purpose or a critical one – as centrally located it is thus difficult to discern an intentional function of the meme as addressing an audience. However, even the memes located in and around the neutral center still inhere aspects of a neo-Dadaist semiotic. As noted earlier, a neo-Dadaist semiotic includes any one or combination of the following: dark humor; distanced irony; disillusionment; horror/shock at the modern age (but with no direct or explicit deliberation on that which horrifies or shocks); bizarre and absurd expressions; self-deprecation; cringe; offensive humor; scatological references. For example, the *White Guy Blinking* meme actually originated as a short looping video or GIF of Drew Scanlon, "a video editor and podcaster at video game website Giant Bomb" (Knowyourmeme. com, 2017). It is normally deployed to show dismay, to express feelings of confusion, disillusionment, or hurt feelings.

What is remarkable about this and related GIFs is the possibility of their communicative *function* without actually knowing the origin of the GIF. This is precisely the point of the neo-Dadaist semiotic: we are inundated with content, messages, information, news, etc. and in the relentless cycle of mediated participation and interaction we have as response options a *readymade* expression, prefabricated and easy to acquire and use. Instead of engaging in conversation, a person can simply access the GIF and deploy it as a substitute for meaningful dialogue. Related to this, the *Roll Safe* meme is an image-macro and features "a screenshot of actor Kayode Ewumi grinning and pointing to his temple while portraying the character Reece Simpson (a.k.a. "Roll Safe") in the web series Hood Documentary" (Knowyourmeme.com, 2016b). In the coordinate plane, I plotted the meme centrally but with a more humorous purpose. As an image-macro, the meme tends to use either one-liners or the set-up and punchline approach. A sample one-liner is *you can't be broke if you don't check your bank account* and a sample set-up and punchline is [top text] *can't get fired* [bottom text, punchline] *if you don't have a job*. The primary function of the meme is arguably to embrace a humorous approach to mistakes in critical thinking and decision-making, but traces of a neo-Dadaist semiotic are present. Depending on the joke, the *Roll Safe* meme includes aspects of dark humor, distanced irony, and by its nature a kind of celebratory self-deprecation, as if to say '*I know I'm not good enough, but it's funny so that's cool*'.

On the left-leaning side, one meme in particular demonstrates a neo-Dadaist semiotic. The *Kendall Jenner, Pepsi* meme emerged from a commercial which was designed to speak to the Black Lives Matter movement but backfired. The commercial itself was pulled due to critical complaints, but it may still be available on YouTube (it is available here through Kendall and Kylie Jenner's YouTube channel: https://www.youtube.com/watch?v=dA5Yq1DLSmQ). Basically, despite other numerous problems, the all-white production team likely had the best of intentions in their work, but without connecting to the Black Lives Matter community, the commercial was destined to inspire memes. Perhaps, the most striking, hypermemetic moment in the commercial was the use of Jenner as a speechless spokesperson for a safely anonymous protest in the commercial (such as the peace signs decorated with the colors of Pepsi's logo, surely not accidental). In the commercial, a fashion photographer is snapping shots of Jenner modeling a metallic-looking dress and wearing a blonde wig. In the background, protestors march by for a purpose not explicitly expressed. Suddenly, Jenner becomes aware of the protest, and oddly tosses her blonde wig toward an unsuspecting black woman without looking at her, wipes off her lipstick, and walks through, among, and toward the front of the crowd toward a (white) police officer. Jenner hands the officer a can of Pepsi, the music track stops to allow for the sound effect of the opening of the can, and the commercial ends as if all has been ameliorated through the sharing of a sweetened, carbonated beverage. I have plotted this as left-leaning and critical arguably for obvious reasons.

However, what aspects of the neo-Dadaist semiotic are present in the meme's derivatives? The commercial was aired on April 4, 2017, and already by the next day individuals levied serious critique on it. Bernice King, daughter of Dr. Martin Luther King, Jr., tweeted a black-and-white image of her father being pushed by police with the text *"If only Daddy would have known about the power of #Pepsi"*, shown in Figure 8.3. Another depicts Dr. King as asking for a six-pack of Pepsi to diffuse anticipated tension in Selma, shown in Figure 8.4. Other remixes depicted Jenner offering the can of Pepsi to a smiling Adolf Hitler ostensibly to diffuse the situation. Another shows a historical image of a black male nonviolent protester sitting in a diner surrounded by young white men staring at him with the text *"Oh nevermind. He ordered a Pepsi"*. Still others continue the trend and leave out Jenner, such as one featuring Malcolm X holding a firearm, peering out a window with the text *"When the cops come and you only got Coca-Cola in the fridge"*. Another meme shows a young black man shouting at police in riot gear with the text *"You want diet or regular Pepsi?"* Similar to related memes which employ historical references the *Kendall Jenner, Pepsi* meme inheres several aspects of a neo-Dadaist semiotic. The commercial is a failure for the purpose intended by Pepsi, but it is a success as it allows individuals to vent their anger and frustration and to do so in creative and image-driven ways.

Simply taking a colorized image of Pepsi can and inserting it into a black-and-white image of Martin Luther King, Jr. or positioning Jenner

Be A King ✔
@BerniceKing

(Follow) ⌄

If only Daddy would have known about the power of #Pepsi.

9:15 AM - 5 Apr 2017

151,250 Retweets **284,187** Likes

◯ 1.6K   ⇄ 151K   ♡ 284K   ✉

Figure 8.3 Bernice King's Tweet in Response to Kendall Jenner Pepsi Ad.

as giving the can to Hitler operates as a visual catachresis. Used in literary and artistic movements, such as Dadaism and Surrealism, catachresis' function is to connote an extreme emotional state or to suggest alienation. In rhetoric, catachresis generally means the intentional misuse of a word such as to refer to a table's *legs* (where *leg* is technically biological but semantically true in context) or to say that an unemployed person is rather a *job-seeker*.

As a visual catachresis within a neo-Dadaist semiotic, the *Kendall Jenner, Pepsi* memes use historical imagery and references in order to elevate the extreme egregiousness of the commercial through the signification of persistent and real-world concerns and issues. The superficial aspect here is humor; despite the memes also, of course, being critical, their capacity for humor should not be overlooked. The humorous component is *superficial* in the *surface* sense of the word. The deeper connotative meaning is much more important. Aside from humor, a semblance

"Aye...tell Jesse to get a 6-pack of Pepsi and bring it to Selma. I'll explain later..."

Figure 8.4 MLK Jr. Needs Pepsi for Selma: Remixing Kendall Jenner Pepsi Ad.

of pain inhabits the remixed responses to the commercial, such as Bernie King's tweet. The *readymade* function of meme persists when an event or issue drives the urge to respond expressly to it. As such, internet memes remain available to quickly encapsulate a critical sentiment visually and meaningfully.

In the coordinate plane overall, memes plotted as leaning politically left tend to function as a visual venting apparatus, one that enables expressions of outrage and disillusionment. Due to the nature of the environment where they are shared (social media platforms) little else is accomplished. Engaging in memetic production and distribution usurps other real-world, community engagement. Admittedly, this is a rather broad generalization, but it proposes a curious outcome. Politically, left-leaning memes serve a venting function, whereas right-leaning memes – despite also providing an opportunity to vent – reconfirm group allegiances visually. One set of memes appears to express irony and frustration, another set of memes seems focused on maintaining the ideological status quo. More empirical data should be collected and analyzed to test this perspective.

With regard to all of the memes included in the coordinate plane, especially those which are initially critical or have the capacity to be remixed critically, the communicative function is restricted to online discursive practice. Sharing such memes helps to reify identity with a group and also addresses a need for social currency, that is, to share such memes for the reactions they will bring. My primary critique of internet memes is that while it may be enjoyable to take part in the spectacle little else appears to be accomplished. It is worthwhile to point out that *microactivism*, or the day-to-day blogging, posting, sharing, etc. on an issue of social import (Marichal, 2013), is one way to understand how spreading memes may at least lead to broadening awareness of an issue and is arguably an inherently good outcome. However, the memes plotted in the coordinate plane point to several serious issues in society (such as racial tensions, questions of white privilege, the rise of the far-right, etc.) but what do individuals achieve in sharing the memes? What is actually gained? In the course of this work, I have addressed, for example, how internet memes may assist in negotiating identity online and how some memes, such as *The Babadook*, perhaps also express support for marginalized groups. Yet, it seems unlikely that individuals or groups will accomplish anything through the critical production and consumption of internet memes unless a community is engaged and plans are made strategically to advance certain political preferences. Social media seems to be excellent at initiating reactions to real-world events, especially ones that trigger political or socio-cultural perspectives or one that polarizes, but exceedingly poor at following through on pursuing actionable social change. Indeed, even as a phrase, *social media* is less accurate when used to describe what it is supposed to signify. Internet memes visually reconfirm biases, allow for people to vent their anger, rage, frustration, etc. without the commitment of engaging in a social movement.

It is my contention that meaningful action and opportunities for social change, regardless of the desired political leaning, is being replaced by a hypermemetic spectacle. The confluence of reacting to real-world events, social and cultural points of interest, political movements, etc. and engaging in online networking means that online discourse is at once liberating and paralyzing. The former emanates from the vast array of communicative tools available to anyone with access, and the latter occurs given that the operation of online spaces is nuanced by malleable truths, tribalism, and emotional rather than logical reasoning. Internet memes are surely only one part of the discursive maelstrom but their tightly encapsulated visual nature is conducive to such a situation.

Concluding Discussion

The major contribution I have attempted to make with this final chapter is to suggest a new way of seeing internet memes entirely, especially those which inhere a critical aspect of the real world. The linkages I have established among Dada, Surrealism, Neue Sachlichkeit, and internet memes are not accidental; rather, they are purposeful. Viewing memes as a new form of cultural and artistic expression gives further meaning and importance to their discursive power in digital culture. Digital culture is perhaps best imagined as a kind of bridge, a connection between the real world of atoms and the digital world of bits. Memes act as signposts of meaning which emerge from individuals interacting with one another in the social system. However, their construction and denotative as well as connotative meaning are impacted by ideological practice. I have insisted throughout this work that ideology, with respect to internet memes, is enacted, is a lived experience, similar to culture in general but with specific reference to the ways meaning and expression can be both constrained and emancipated through discourse. The advantage of viewing Dadaism, for example, as an early conceptual reference point for internet memes helps elucidate contemporary choices to deploy memes largely in reaction or response to real-world events. The tendency for hypermemetic expressions means a great amount of attention is spent on producing, curating, and consumption memes and their messages, but likely doing little about the problems or crises indicated in the memes.

References

Benjamin, W. (1969/1935). The work of art in the age of mechanical reproduction. In H. Zohn (Trans.) & H. Arendt (Ed.), *Illuminations* (pp. 1–26). New York: Schocken Books.

Criado, E. (2014, October 15). Black Pete: 'Cheese-face' to partially replace blackface during Dutch festivities. *The Independent*. Retrieved from https://www.independent.co.uk/news/world/europe/black-pete-cheese-face-to-partially-replace-blackface-during-dutch-festivities-9794880.html

Crilly, R. (2015, November 26). Donald Trump accused of mocking disabled reporter. *The Telegraph*. Retrieved from: https://www.telegraph.co.uk/news/worldnews/donald-trump/12019097/Donald-Trump-accused-of-mocking-disabled-reporter.html

Dabringer, W., Figlhuber, G., & Guserl, S. (2015). *Formen und Funktionen bildender Kunst 2*. Vienna: Verlag Hölder-Pichler-Tempsky GmbH.

Duchamp, M. (1961, October 19). *The art of assemblage: A symposium*. New York: The Museum of Modern Art. Retrieved from https://www.moma.org/learn/moma_learning/themes/dada/marcel-duchamp-and-the-readymade

Goff, P. A., Eberhardt, J. L., Williams, M. J., & Jackson, M. C. (2008). Not yet human: Implicit knowledge, historical dehumanization, and contemporary consequences. *Journal of Personality and Social Psychology, 94*(2), 292–306. doi:10.1037/0022-3514.94.2.292

Hoins, M. (2016, February 23). "Neo-Dadaism": Absurdist humor and the millennial generation. Retrieved from https://medium.com/@meganhoins/neo-dadaism-absurdist-humor-and-the-millennial-generation-f27a39bcf321

Horwitz, R. P. (Ed.). (2001). *The American studies anthology.* Lanham, MD: SR Books.

Hopkins, D. (2004). *Dada and surrealism.* New York: Oxford University Press.

Jacobs, J., & Pettypiece, S. (2018, March 2). Trump swaps his beloved burgers for salads and soups in new diet. *Bloomberg.* Retrieved from https://www. bloomberg.com/news/articles/2018-03-02/trump-swaps-his-beloved-burgers-for-salads-and-soups-in-new-diet

Jenkins, H. (2012). *Textual poachers: Television fans and participatory culture.* New York: Routledge.

Knowyourmeme.com. (2016a). *Harambe.* Retrieved from https://knowyourmeme. com/memes/harambe-the-gorilla

Knowyourmeme.com. (2016b). *Roll safe.* Retrieved from https://knowyourmeme. com/memes/roll-safe

Knowyourmeme.com. (2017). *Drew Scanlon reaction* [White guy blinks meme]. Retrieved from https://knowyourmeme.com/memes/drew-scanlon-reaction

Lewis, P., & Hilder, P. (2018, March 23). Leaked: Cambridge Analytica's blueprint for Trump victory. *The Guardian.* Retrieved from https://www.theguardian. com/uk-news/2018/mar/23/leaked-cambridge-analyticas-blueprint-for-trump-victory#img-2

Marichal, J. (2013). Political Facebook groups: Micro-activism and the digital front stage. *First Monday, 18,* Article 12.

McCausland, P. (2017, July 2). Pepe the frog creator wants to make him a symbol of peace and love. *NBC News.* Retrieved from http://www.nbcnews.com/news/ us-news/pepe-frog-creator-wants-make-him-symbol-peace-love-n779101

McCormick, R. (2009). Coming out of the uniform: Political and sexual emancipation in Leotine Sagan's *Mädchen in Uniform* (1931). In N. Isenberg (Ed.), *Weimar cinema: An essential guide to classic films of the era* (pp. 271–289). New York: Columbia University Press.

Milner, R. M. (2012). *The world made meme: Discourse and identity in participatory media* (PhD thesis). University of Kansas, Lawrence, KS. Retrieved from https://kuscholarworks.ku.edu/handle/1808/10256

Milner, R. (2013). Hacking the social: Internet memes, identity antagonism, and the logic of lulz. *Fibreculture Journal, 22*(156), 62–92. Retrieved from http:// twentytwo.fibreculturejournal.org/fcj-156-hacking-the-social-internet-memes-identity-antagonism-and-the-logic-of-lulz/#comment-20

MoMA (Museum of Modern Art). (2018). *Marcel Duchamp and the ready-made.* Retrieved from https://www.moma.org/learn/moma_learning/themes/ dada/marcel-duchamp-and-the-readymade

Nahon, K., & Hemsley, J. (2013). *Going viral.* Cambridge: Polity Press.

Open Culture (2011, June 24). Andy Warhol eats a Burger King Whopper, and we watch ... and watch. *Open Culture: Art, Film, Food & Drink.* Retrieved from http://www.openculture.com/2011/06/andy_warhol_eats_a_burger_and_we_watch_and_watch.html

Phillips, W., & Milner, R. (2017). *The ambivalent internet: Mischief, oddity, and antagonism online.* Cambridge: Polity Press.

Richter, H. (1965). *Dada: Art and anti-art (world of art).* London: Thames and Hudson Ltd.

Sanouillet, M., & Peterson, E. (Eds.). (1973). *The writings of Marcel Duchamp.* New York: Oxford University Press.

Shifman, L. (2013). Memes in a digital world: Reconciling with a conceptual troublemaker. *Journal of Computer-Mediated Communication, 18*, 362–377.

Shifman, L. (2014). *Memes in digital culture.* Cambridge: MIT Press.

de Telegraaf (2013, October 22). *VN wil einde Sinterklaasfeest.* Retrieved from https://www.telegraaf.nl/nieuws/1043077/vn-wil-einde-sinterklaasfeest

Tan, G., & Porzecanski, K. (2018, December 03). Wall Street rule for the #MeToo era: Avoid women at all cost. *Bloomberg.* Retrieved from https://www.bloomberg.com/news/articles/2018-12-03/a-wall-street-rule-for-the-metoo-era-avoid-women-at-all-cost

Transcript (2017). *America first, Netherlands second.* Retrieved from http://lybio.net/america-first-netherlands-second/entertainment/

Postface/Afterword

Throughout this work, I have described the communicative function of internet memes as a discursive power and that this is conceptually comprised of ideology, semiotics, and intertextuality. I maintain that internet memes possess the capacity for discursive power but that this is dependent upon whether an individual or group receives the preferred reading of the meme-as-message in the way intended. Complicating matters of reception is the incorporation of media narratives in memes; whether humorous or critical, memes that address a real-world event or issue must also incorporate one or more references to the reported news story. Yet, this is already a fragmented process because the news story itself invariably contains constructed traces to the original source presented in the form of interesting and possibly entertaining mediated information. The paradox of internet memes is that, on the one hand, they are remarkably robust units of digital culture whose utility resides in their communicative function. However, on the other hand, this function also constrains, delimits, and frames how individuals view and think about real-world events and issues. One major cause for this is the structure of social media platforms. Designed to keep individuals engaged for as much time as possible, social media applications offer users an experience mediated by images, hashtags, tags, and related tactics driving the strategic usurpation of attention. Facebook, Twitter, Instagram, Snapchat, and other applications possess unique character-istics which differentiate them from each other. However, they seem to share one critical quality. It is as if all social media platforms had been designed with Wilbur Schramm's *fraction of selection* in mind, as if social media engineers purposefully constructed social apps to maxi-mize the perceived rewards of use and minimize the effort required to gain the reward, thus densely increasing frequency of use. Rewards of use vary depending on the issue and the individual but could include any one or more of the following: desire to be liked, self-affirmation; commercial gain; romance; obfuscation and inveiglement; eliminating boredom; maintaining addiction; keeping current with one's network and/or general or specific news stories, and more. With billions of people using social media on a daily basis, it is not surprising that internet memes are useful in quick and succinct albeit ideologically driven visual arguments. Of course, rational debate is still possible but is threatened by the communicative alacrity afforded by internet memes. Considering how the internet meme has been analyzed and unpacked throughout this work, its impact on discourse should not be underestimated.

Index

Note: Boldface page numbers refer to tables; italic page numbers refer to figures and page numbers followed by "n" denote endnotes.

Printed in the United States
by Baker & Taylor Publisher Services